REVIEWING THE REVIEW: SPECIAL FOCUS ON THE STANDARD OF REVIEW IN THE BARAYAGWIZA CASE

REVIEWING THE REVIEW: SPECIAL FOCUS ON THE STANDARD OF REVIEW IN THE BARAYAGWIZA CASE

Gracieux Mbuzukongira

GALDA VERLAG 2023

Bibliografische Information der Deutschen Nationalbibliothek
Die Deutsche Nationalbibliothek verzeichnet diese Publikation in der Deutschen Nationalbibliografie; detaillierte bibliografische Daten sind im Internet über https://dnb.de abrufbar.

ISBN 978-3-96203-310-1 (Print)
ISBN 978-3-96203-311-8 (E-Book)

Until justice becomes perfected, unworthy judges who administer faulty judgments are the prime cause of immorality and exile.

[Likutey Kalakhot III, p. 110 a]

TABLE OF CONTENT

ACKNOWLEDGEMENTS

Part of this research has been conducted at the Max-Planck-Institute for Comparative Public and International Law in Heidelberg, I take this opportunity to thank the Directors of the Institute, Professor Armin von Bogdandy and Professor Anne Peters for having opened the doors of the Institute for me once again and allowing me to gather the needed materials for this research at the Institute.

In a special way I want to thank His Excellency Ambassador Mohammed Sani and Professor Mathias Sahinkuye of the African Institute of International Law in Arusha for having welcomed me at their Institute and having allowed me access at their various resources as well.

My few years of academic profession have met high and low seasons. However Emeritus Bishop Professor Owdenburg Mdegella of the Evangelical Lutheran Church of Tanzania- Iringa Diocese has stood with me throughout. May you find my heartfelt thanks here, for having been such an inspiration.

I thank my family for having been supportive. I thank my wife Bébé L. Mahekay, who has always been there for us raising men and women worth the next generation.

INTRODUCTION

Born in Commune Mutura, Prefecture de Gisenyi, in the Republic of Rwanda, Mr. Jean Bosco Barayagwiza held the post of Director of Political Affairs at the Ministry of Foreign Affairs.[1] He was initially arrested by the Cameroonian authorities, following requests of the governments of Belgium and Rwanda.[2]

However, after a lengthy legal process, the Cameroonian Court of Appeal rejected the extradition request from the Rwandese government and ordered the release of the accused. On the day, the Court of Appeal ordered his release, the ICTR Prosecutor requested his provisional detention as a new procedure was initiated under the ICTR laws.

Indeed, on 15.04.1996, the authorities of Cameroon arrested and detained Mr. Barayagwiza and several other suspects on suspicion of having committed genocide and crimes against humanity in Rwanda in 1994, and on 17.04.1996, the Prosecutor requested that provisional measures pursuant to Rule 40 be taken concerning Barayagwiza.

According to Rule 40(a):

> In case of urgency, the Prosecutor may request any State:
>
> (i) To arrest a suspect and place him in custody;
>
> (ii) To seize all physical evidence;
>
> (iii) To take all necessary measures to prevent the escape of a suspect or an accused, injury to or intimidation of a victim or witness, or the destruction of evidence. The State concerned shall comply forthwith, in accordance with Article 28 of the Statute.

On 6.05.1996, the Prosecutor asked Cameroon for a three-week extension of the detention of all the suspects, including Mr. Barayagwiza. However, on 16.05.1996, the Prosecutor informed Cameroon that she only

---

1 ICTR, Prosecutor v. Barayagwiza, Appeals Chamber, Judgment of 28.11.2007, para 3

2 ICTR, Prosecutor v. Barayagwiza, Trial Chamber II, Decision on the extremely urgent motion by the defense for orders to review and/or nullify the arrest and provisional detention of the suspect, 17 Nov 1998, P 4

intended to pursue prosecutions against four of the detainees, excluding Mr Barayagwiza.[3]

On 21.02.1997 when the Court of Appeal of Cameroon rejected the Rwandan extradition request and ordered the release of the suspects, including Mr. Barayagwiza. The same day, the Prosecutor requested for his provisional detention according to Rule 40 and he was re-arrested the same day according to this Order.

Pursuant to rule 40(a) *bis* of the Rules according to which: "In the conduct of an investigation, the Prosecutor may transmit to the Registrar, for an order by a Judge assigned pursuant to Rule 28, a request for the transfer to and provisional detention of a suspect in the premises of the detention unit of the Tribunal…" The Prosecutor requested an Order for arrest and transfer of Mr. Barayagwiza on 24 February 1997 and on 3 March 1997, however, he was not transferred to the ICTR until 19 November 1997, and his initial appearance did not take place until 23 February 1998.

On 24.02.1998, the Appellant filed the Extremely Urgent Motion seeking to have his arrest and detention nullified. The arguments of the parties were heard on 11.09.1998. Trial Chamber II, in its Decision of 17.11.1998, dismissed the Extremely Urgent Motion *in toto*.[4]

On 27.11.1998, Mr. Barayagwiza appealed against The Trial Chamber's dismissal of the extremely urgent motion; the Appeals Chamber in its Decision of 3.11.1999 dismissed the indictment and directed immediate release of Mr. Barayagwiza.

However, on the 1.12.1999, the Prosecutor filed a motion for review, and indeed in an unprecedented turn of events, on 31.03.2000 the Appeals Chamber differently composed reviewed its own decision of 3.11.1999 and replaced its dispositions by rejecting the application by Mr. Barayagwiza to be released and decided that for the violation of his rights, he will be entitled to a financial remedy if he is found not guilty, and would he be found guilty his sentence shall be reduced to take into account the violation of his rights.[5]

According to Article 25 of the Statute: "Where a new fact has been discovered which was not known at the time of the proceedings before the Trial Chambers or the Appeals Chamber and which could have been a decisive factor in reaching the decision, the convicted person or the Prosecutor may

3 ICTR, Prosecutor v. Barayagwiza, Appeals Chamber, Decision, 3 Nov 1999, para 5
4 Idem para 10
5 Appeals Chamber Decision (Prosecutor's request for review or reconsideration) of 31.03. 2000 para 75

submit to the International Tribunal for Rwanda an application for review of the judgment."

Whereas rule 120 of the Rules provides that: "Where a new fact has been discovered which was not known to the moving party at the time of the proceedings before a Chamber and could not have been discovered through the exercise of due diligence, the defense or, within one year after the final judgment has been pronounced; the Prosecutor, may make a motion to that Chamber, if it can be reconstituted or, failing that, to the appropriate Chamber of the Tribunal for review of the judgment."

Rule 121 of Rules says that: "If the Chamber which ruled on the matter decides that the new fact if it had been proven, could have been a decisive factor in reaching a decision, the Chamber shall review the judgment, and pronounce a further judgment after hearing the parties."

As Mr. Barayagwiza was committed to trial, The Trial Chamber found him Guilty of Conspiracy to Commit Genocide (Count 1), Guilty of Genocide (Count 2), Not Guilty of Complicity in Genocide (Count 3), Guilty of Direct and Public Incitement to Commit Genocide (Count4), Guilty of Crimes against Humanity (Extermination) (Count 5), Not Guilty of Crimes Against Humanity (Murder)(Count 6), Guilty of Crimes against Humanity (Persecution)(Count 7), Not guilty of serious violations of Article 3 Common to the Geneva Conventions and of Additional Protocol ll (Count 8), Not Guilty of Serious Violations of Article 3 Common to the Geneva Conventions and the Additional Protocol II (Count 9)[6]

Nevertheless, the Appeals Chambers reversed the decision of the Trial Chamber based on Article 6(1) of the Statute for the crimes of direct and public incitement to commit genocide for his acts within the CDR and conspiracy to commit genocide, as well as his convictions based on Article 6(3) of the Statute in respect of his acts within RTLM and the CDR for the crimes of genocide, direct and public incitement to commit genocide, and extermination and persecution as crimes against humanity.[7]

The appeals Chamber rather affirmed the convictions of Mr. Banyagwiza according to Article 6(l) of the Statute for (1) having instigated the commission of genocide by CDR members and *Impuzamugambi* in Kigali; (2) having ordered or instigated the commission of extermination as a crime against humanity by CDR members and *Impuzamugambi* in Kigali, (3) having

6 Trial Chamber Judgment,03.12.2003, para 1093

7 ICTR, Prosecutor v. Barayagwiza, Appeals Chamber Judgment, 28.11.2007, page 345

instigated the commission of persecution as a crime against humanity by CDR members and *Impuzamugambi* in Kigali.[8]

1. The Judge made Law Theory

The question of the role of the judge would appear to have been decisively dealt with in the jurisprudence and legal theory debates of the seventeenth and eighteenth century yet the case at hand might require us to revisit the same particularly when one considers Maximiliano Hernández Marcos worries as he raises the question that could be generated not only by unequal but also sometimes contradictory decisions or even jurisdictional conflicts between overlapping courts involved in the similar cases.[9]

Indeed whereas the jurisprudence of the International Court of Justice as it will be discussed further, has adopted a strict interpretation of the law on the procedure for review in international law, the ad-hoc tribunals for the former Yugoslavia and Rwanda have adopted a lenient interpretation of the concept leading to a conflicting stand vis-à-vis the jurisprudence of the International Court of Justice.

Such a situation brings back the discussion on the role of the judge within the law-making process its limits and contours. Indeed whereas the introduction to the study of jurisprudence of Nathaniel Lindley notes that the lawgiver must always until the contrary is shown to be the case be presumed to have expressed himself correctly and therefore in case of doubt is to be considered as having enacted everything logically implied by the words he has used.[10] However Chief Justice Sir Matthew Hale, suggests that the law is to accommodate the conditions, exigencies, and conveniences of the people through those exigencies and conveniences do insensibly grow upon the people, so many times there grows insensibly a variation of laws, especially in a long tract of time.[11] He further argues that the law will maintain itself as a system while changing over long periods through a buildup of precedents.[12]

---

8 Idem, page 346

9 Maximiliano Hernández Marcos, Conceptual Aspects of Legal Enlightenment in Europe in Patrick Riley, A treatise of legal philosophy and general jurisprudence, the philosophers" philosophy of law from the seventeenth century to our days, Springer, 2009, p 84

10 Nathaniel Lindley, An introduction to the study of jurisprudence, Hodges and Smith, 1955, p 4

11 Suri Ratnapala, Jurisprudence, Cambridge University Press, 2009, p 271

12 Idem

Such change might be a result of the change of the law by the lawgiver, either the parliament or the King or rather the State as the same might be brought about by the judge by way of interpretation as hereunder discussed.

The question might appear to have been settled however it once was subject to fierce debate. Citing Cattaneo and Salvador-Coderch, Maximiliano Hernández Marcos recalls that the interpretation was no longer understood as a valid normative-juridical source that was an alternative in cases of doubt or legal vacuum, and began to be perceived in the opposite sense, but with an unfavorable connotation as a spurious activity of legal creation that undermined the faculty of juridical creation recognized exclusively in the sovereign legislator.[13]

Viewed negatively, the judge would seem to be confined by their original task namely the implementation of the law, and abstain from any contribution toward the making of the same, thus the judge would consider the law as a final product to which they are required to apply as it is without any addition or diminution.

Such a school of thought will find its applicability in the theory of literal interpretation of the law. This is understood as referring to the law only by assigning to the concept its ordinary meaning in its application by the judge. This view is however challenged by the fact that a time the law could be couched using ambiguous or less explicit words sometimes even obscure terms which would require the intervention of the judge either through their interpretation by assigning to certain words a meaning which resonates with the understanding of the judge when a contentious case is brought before or such meaning can be given through an advisory opinion when such opinion is sought by any interested party.

The discussion could be dismissed for its anachronic nature, as one might recall the struggle against "the despotism of the courts" entailed throughout the second half of the 18th century and the proposal of two fundamental remedies:

> On the one hand, in opposition to the usual recourse by judges to the *interpretatio doctrinalis* of scholars and jurists, the literal single interpretation of the law was advocated, and,

[13] Maximiliano Hernández Marcos, Conceptual Aspects of Legal Enlightenment in Europe in Patrick Riley, A treatise of legal philosophy and general jurisprudence, the philosophers" philosophy of law from the seventeenth century to our days, Springer, 2009, p 84

> on the other hand, where the law was not clear or there was a legal vacuum, the *interpretatio authentica* was proposed as the only legitimate one and, with it the institution of the recourse to the legislator.[14]

However the failure of these two prelates which sought to strictly contain the judge within a limited sphere of simple application of the law, that is the judge will be called upon to simply apply the law as given nothing more. This position will nevertheless be challenged by many situations including the reality that the word of a given text could change its meaning with time, and that certain situations or inventions that came into existence after the adoption of the law would hardly fit in such strict textualization, doctrine.

Words within the context of law indeed convey the meaning that they carry at the time of the adoption of the law hence the need of referring to a legal basis when adjudicating, it becomes problematic when the scrupulous application of a text defeat the comprehensive purpose of the entire law seen from a macroscopic viewpoint. Thus as said by Antonin Scalia and Bryan Garner "the words of a governing text are of paramount concern, and what they convey, in their context, is what the text means."[15]

It is at this point that the judge is liberated from a textual application of the law and is rather invited to contextualize the words even if the process might imply assigning to the text a purposeful meaning for it to fit in the context. Thus through an interpretation that may be referred to confirm the ordinary meaning of the terms used in their context or to determine the meaning when the application of the rule of interpretation referred to above leaves the meaning ambiguous or obscure or leads to a result that is manifestly absurd or unreasonable.[16]

Perhaps the role of the judge will become even more absolute when they are called upon to issue an advisory opinion of a given legal text, which task is never expected of the lawmakers but rather to the judge who then will apply their skills to interpret the said text.

---

14 Maximiliano Hernández Marcos, Conceptual Aspects of Legal Enlightenment in Europe in Patrick Riley, A treatise of legal philosophy and general jurisprudence, the philosophers" philosophy of law from the seventeenth century to our days, Springer, 2009, p 90

15 Antonin Scalia and Bryan A. Garner, Reading Law, The Interpretation of Legal Texts, Thomson/West, 2012, p 66

16 Nihal Jayawickrama, the judicial application of human rights law: National, Regional, and International Jurisprudence, Cambridge University Press, 2002, 161

It can then be concluded that the stigma of legal uncertainty which enlightened thinkers hurled against the judicial interpretation while the other consisted of the denunciation of the usurpation of the legislative power that legally corresponded only to the sovereign finds no justification in the legal practice, neither should be seen as a violation of the principle of separation of powers as taught by Jean Jacques Rousseau.

As indicated by Lord Wensleydale in re: Grey v. Pearson:

> [I]n construing . . . all written instruments, the grammatical and ordinary sense of the words is to be adhered to unless that would lead to some absurdity, or some repugnance or inconsistency with the rest of the instrument, in which case the grammatical and ordinary sense of the words may be modified, to avoid that absurdity and inconsistency, but no farther.[17]

2. Research Methods

It should be indicated that as far as research methods is concerned, this research will take two approaches: a theoretical approach reflecting on the actual creation of legal rules; and an implementation-focused approach, reflecting on the observance and application of legal rules and the successes achieved in strengthening legality and for consolidating law.[18]

As defined by Banakar and Travers[19], the rule-based paradigm which consists of a study of law with recourse to the exegesis authoritative argument that allows one to read and criticize its content will be of great use for this research.

The study's focus will be doctrinal, analyzing legal sources available within the United Nations Mechanism for International Criminal Tribunals (UN-MICT) and its valuable resources. The research will also be based on other sources, especially scholarly writings published in leading international and national periodicals, journals, newspapers, reports, Aide-Mémoire, Travaux Préparatoires, reference works, and other relevant data available.

---

17 *Grey v. Pearson,*[1857] 6 H.L. Cas. 61, 106

18 See Dzhangir Kerimov, *Methodology of Law*, Progress Publishers, 1989, p 12

19 Reza Banakar and Max Travers, Law, Sociology and Method, *Theory and Method in Socio-Legal Research*, Hart Publishing, 2005, p 8

3. The Structure of the Research

This research is divided into two parts. Its first part which comprises of the first two chapters discusses the procedural aspect of the Barayagwiza trial. It focuses the discussion on the doctrine of review of a court's decision in general and in particular how such doctrine applies in the context of criminal proceedings. The discussion will be focused on the required standard of its application and it will be mirrored to the case at hand.

The second part which comprises of the last two chapters is focused on the substantive part of the judgment as it focuses more on the crimes for which Mr. Baragwiza was found guilty by the Trial Chamber.

A special discussion will be devoted to the crime of genocide as contextualized in this particular case and on that occasion the crime of conspiracy to commit genocide will be elaborated more as an inchoate crime, followed by a discussion on the crime of incitement to commit genocide.

The prohibition to commit genocide is considered part of international customary law,[20] such crime must be thoroughly studied first from a theoretical viewpoint as well as various difficulties it raises during the trial.

[20] David Boyle, Genocide et crimes contre l'humanite: Convergences et divergences, in La justice penale internationale dans les decisions des tribunaux ad hoc: etudes des law clinics en droit penal international Dalloz, 2003, p 134

CHAPTER 1

THE DOCTRINE OF JUDICIAL REVIEW IN INTERNATIONAL LAW

1.1 Definition and Condition of Applicability

The 1899 Convention for the Pacific Settlement of International Disputes is among the early treaties which provided for a possible review if a party to the proceeding is not satisfied by the given Award. However, the 1899 Convention applies within the context of arbitration. Indeed article 55 provides that: "on the ground of the discovery of some new facts calculated to exercise a decisive influence on the award, and which, at the time of the discussion was closed, was unknown to the tribunal and the party demanding revision." Later the same provision will be couched by Article 83 of the 1907 Hague Convention for Pacific Settlement of International Disputes mutatis mutandis.

The spirit of this provision will be captured by article 61 of the Statute of the Permanent Court of International Justice which will coincidentally become article 61 (1) of the Statute of the International Court of Justice according to which:

> An application for revision of a judgment can be made only when it is based upon the discovery of some fact of such a nature as to be a decisive factor, which fact was, when the judgment was given, unknown to the Court and also to the party claiming revision, always provided that such ignorance was not due to negligence.

This research will be squared within the framework of the review of a judgment or any other order taken by a court or a tribunal as opposed to the process of judicial review which is understood as a review of a decision of a legislative, executive, or administrative body against which a given applicant seeks a review of court.

Indeed in El Salvador v Honduras, citing the Award of 1921 in the Jean-Guillaume Krichel case before the mixed arbitral tribunal, Honduras' response to the application for review indicated that:

> La procédure en révision a été créée pour remédier à l'ignorance dans laquelle pouvaient se trouver les intéressés en ce qui concerne un fait déterminant existant déjà antérieurement à la clôture des débats et qui, s'il avait été porté à la connaissance des juges, aurait pu exercer une influence décisive sur leur décision.[21]

Thus the procedure of review can be understood as a remedial procedure through which a party is allowed to request the court or tribunal to reopen its earlier decision upon discovery of new facts under the conditions determined by the law as it is hereunder discussed. It should be stressed that such a legal process is accepted only before the court or tribunal which took the decision for which revision is sought.

1.2 Conditions

1.2.1 Discovery of New Facts

What needs to be considered as a new fact was discussed at length in the application for review of the judgment of 11.07.1996 in the case concerning the application of the convention on the prevention and punishment of the crime of genocide. As Judge Koroma pointed out the revision procedure is essentially about newly discovered facts or arguments and as such it is not about a legal challenge.[22]

Thus Judge Vereshchetin[23] in his dissenting opinion suggested rather a literal understanding of the concept of fact before it is contextualized in the case, amongst other definitions he suggests the definition of a fact as "a finding of fact as an assertion that a phenomenon exists, has existed or will exist,

[21] Cour International de Justice, Affaire de la demande en revision de l'arret du 11 Septembre 1992 en l'affaire du differend frontalier terrestre, insulaire et maritime (El Salvador c. Hondras; Nicaragua (intervenant) Observation ecrites du gouvernement de Honduras, para 53

[22] Separate opinion Koroma, para 2

[23] Dissenting opinion of Judge Vereshchetin, para 10

independently of any assertion as to its legal effect."[24] He further suggests the definition given by the Concise Oxford Dictionary according to which a fact is a "thing certainly known to have occurred or be true"[25] whereas Judge Mahiou will define the concept as: "[A]n event which occurred, which took place at a given point in time."[26]

If the concept of fact could be easily understood it needs to be indicated that as said by Judge Mahiou the question is not the fact itself which is inherently or objectively new, it is the knowledge of that fact that must be new to the party relying upon it or to the court which handed down the judgment.[27]

In the same context, much that ad hoc Judge Dimitrijevic does not agree with the reference to the dictionary meaning of the concept of "fact," he raises a pertinent question of the duality between the existence of a fact and its discovery or determination. Indeed the concept of new fact could be understood as a fact that existed at the time when the judgment was given, but which was unknown to the court and to the party claiming revision, or a realization that occurred after the judgment was delivered and showing that the "old" fact, which had been assumed to exist at the time of the judgment, had not existed or that a fact which had not been seen as existing or had been misinterpreted as such, had existed at the relevant time.[28]

Judge Dimitrijevic concludes that whereas paragraph 1 of article 61 provides that an application for revision of a judgment may be made only when it is based upon the discovery of some fact which was unknown to the Court and also to the party claiming revision when the judgment was given

---

24 De Smith, Woolf& Jowell, Judicial Review of Administrative Action, 5th ed, p 277, para 5-079

25 The Concise Oxford Dictionary of Current English, 6th ed, p 370

26 See International Court of Justice, Application for review of the judgment of 11 July 1996 in the case concerning the application of the convention on the prevention and punishment of the crime of genocide, separate opinion Judge Mahiou para 2

27 Para 6 the same has been referred to in the Honduras submission indicating that: "ce qui est proprement « nouveau », ce n'est pas le fait mais la connaissance qu'on en a. Le fait, quant à lui, existait déjà antérieurement au prononcé de l'arrêt. Sinon, il ne pourrait pas,par définition, présenter cet autre caractère requis de l'article 61, son caractère « déterminant » pour l'arrêt de la Cour. Ce qui rend le fait « nouveau », c'est sa découverte, non son existence. Il existait tout aussi bien avant qu'après le prononcé de l'arrêt au fond, mais il était resté inconnu de la Cour comme des parties." See International Court of Justice, Application for Revision of the Judgment of 11 September 1992 in the Case concerning the Land, Island and Maritime Frontier Dispute (El Salvador/Honduras: Nicaragua intervening) (El Salvador v. Honduras), Written Observations of the Government of Honduras at 2.23

28 See International Court of Justice, Application for Revision of the Judgment of 11 September 1992 in the Case concerning the Land, Island and Maritime Frontier Dispute (El Salvador/Honduras: Nicaragua intervening) (El Salvador v. Honduras), para 11

refers to a fact which existed at the time when the Judgment was given, but which was unknown to the Court and the party claiming revision.

He further submits that paragraph 2 of the same article according to which the proceedings for revision shall be opened by a judgment of the court expressly recording the existence of the new fact, recognizing that it has such a character as to lay the case open to revision refers to a fact which had not existed, or that such fact which had not been seen as existing or had been misinterpreted as such, had existed at the relevant time.

1.2.2 Ratio Decidendi

In its judgment of 18.12.2003, the ICJ found that; the facts asserted by the applicant were not "decisive factors" in respect of the Judgment which it sought to have revised.[29]

Indeed on 10.09.2002, El Salvador filed a request for revision of the Judgment delivered on 11.09.1992 by a Chamber of the Court in the case concerning the Land, Island and Maritime Frontier Dispute (El Salvador/ Honduras: Nicaragua intervening).[30] The application indicated that: "The sole purpose of the application is to seek revision of the course of the boundary decided by the Court for the sixth disputed sector of the land boundary between El Salvador and Honduras."

Whereas in its judgment the Court had held that there was no scientific evidence that the previous course of the Goascoran was such that it debouched in the Estero La Cuth, rather than in any of the other neighboring inlets in the coastline, such as the Estero El Coyol.[31]

In its application, El Salvador submitted that it now has scientific, technical, and historical evidence that there was an abrupt change in the course of the river Goascoran, possibly caused by a cyclone in 1762. El Salvador submitted that this change is the "avulsion" that the Chamber would have been willing to acknowledge had it been proven.[32]

---

[29] Idem, para 40, and para 55

[30] See International Court of Justice, Application for Revision of the Judgment of 11 September 1992 in the Case concerning the Land, Island and Maritime Frontier Dispute (El Salvador/Honduras: Nicaragua intervening) (El Salvador v. Honduras)

[31] See International Court of Justice, Application for Revision of the Judgment of 11 September 1992 in the Case concerning the Land, Island and Maritime Frontier Dispute (El Salvador/Honduras: Nicaragua intervening) (El Salvador v. Honduras), Judgement para 309

[32] See International Court of Justice, Application for Revision of the Judgment of 11 September 1992 in the Case concerning the Land, Island and Maritime Frontier Dispute (El Salvador/Honduras: Nicaragua intervening) (El Salvador v. Honduras), El-Salvador application para 44

Reponding to El Salvador's application, Honduras asked the question: "La Cour aurait-elle raisonné autrement qu'elle l'a fait si elle avait eu connaissance, antérieurement à son jugement, de faits don't elle n'a eu connaissance que par la suite?[33] In other words, would the Court have reasoned differently would it have known facts that it obtained later before its judgment?

Perhaps to answer this question, one might need to adopt Judge Paolilo methodology. In his dissenting opinion ad hoc Judge Paolilo states that it is particularly important for ascertaining whether the new facts presented by the party seeking revision are "of such a nature as to be a decisive factor". That phrase has to be construed as meaning that, if the facts had been known previously, the Chamber would have taken a different decision.[34]

He further advises that it is critical during the process of considering an application for revision of a judgment to properly identify the real *ratio decidendi* of the judgment.[35] It is important to identify the decisive factors of a given judgment then and only then one can assess if any given new fact would have had a *ratio decidendi* on the outcome of the case. To put it differently, which element(s) dictates the decision of the judge in a given has a serious implication in deciding if such fact(s) could warrant the decision of revision of the previous decision.

This condition is indeed critical considering that even if other conditions are met it would serve no purpose if an application for review is granted in case which will end up with the same decision as the reviewed decision. This explains why an application for review should be granted only if the court is convinced that the *ratio decidendi* threshold has been met. Although it should be stressed that this position should not be construed as to mean that once the application for review has been granted the reviewing body must end up with a different judgment. The reviewing judge will assess the facts independently from any previous decision.

1.2.3 Negligence

In the case, Continental Shelf Tunisia v. Libya Arab Jamahiriya, Tunisia would apply for revision and interpretation of the judgment of 24.02.1982.[36]

---

33 Cour International de Justice, Affaire de la demande en revision de l'arret du 11 Septembre 1992 en l'affaire du differend frontalier terrestre, insulaire et maritime (El Salvador c. Hondras; Nicaragua (intervenant) Observation ecrites du gouvernement de Honduras, para 2.25

34 Idem, para 4

35 idem

36 See Application for revision and interpretation of the Judgment of 24 February 1982 in the case concerning the Continental Shelf (Tunisia v. Libyan Arab Jamahiriya) Judgment of 10 December 1985

Indeed Tunisia submitted that the text of a Resolution of the Libyan Council of Ministers of 28.o3.1968, which determined the "real course" of the north-western boundary of a petroleum concession granted by Libya and referred to in the 1982 Judgment, known as Concession No. 137 was unknown to the Court and to the applicant,[37] and as such it could have influenced the outcome of the decision of the Court hence the application for review.

Libya responded by disputing the admissibility of the application contending that "the fact relied on was known to Tunisia, either at the time of the 1982 Judgment or at some time earlier than six months before the filing of the Application for revision, that if the fact was unknown to Tunisia, that ignorance was due to negligence on the part of Tunisia; and that Tunisia has failed to show that the fact discovered was "of such a nature as to be a decisive factor".

The Court cited the Fisheries case, in which the United Kingdom denied knowledge of a Norwegian Decree of 1869 concerning the delimitation of the territorial sea, the Court observed that "As a coastal State on the North Sea, greatly interested in the fisheries in this area, as a maritime Power traditionally concerned with the law of the sea and concerned particularly to defend the freedom of the seas, the United Kingdom could not have been ignorant of the Decree of 1869."[38]

Further, the Court will hold that "normal diligence would require that, when sending a delegation for negotiation of the continental shelf delimitation, following the grant by each side of neighboring or conflicting concessions, a State should first try to learn the exact coordinates of the other party's concession." The Court found that it is also to be expected that, in litigation the ultimate purpose of which is the establishment of a continental shelf delimitation, and in the course of which a petroleum concession in the relevant area is described by one party without precision, the other party will not limit itself to commenting on the matter in its pleading, but itself seek out the information.[39]

The Court concluded that in that case, the fact that the concession boundary coordinates were obtainable by Tunisia, and the fact that it was in its interests to ascertain them, together signify that one of the essential conditions of admissibility of a request for revision laid down in paragraph 1 of Article 61 of the Statute, namely ignorance of a new fact not due to negligence, is

---

[37] Idem, para 11

[38] Idem

[39] Idem, para 27

lacking.[40] It thus could be understood that if an applicant would have fallen short of the normal standard applied for normal due diligence such a State might be considered negligent.

Another case worth mentioning as far as a review at the ICJ is concerned is rather the application for review received by the International Court of Justice in the case Malaysia v. Singapore. Indeed on 2.02.2017, Malaysia filed an Application for revision of the Judgment rendered by the Court on 23.05.2008 in the case concerning Sovereignty over Pedra Branca/Pulau Batu Puteh, Middle Rocks, and South Ledge (Malaysia/Singapore).[41] However on 28.05.2018, Malaysia notified the Court that the parties have agreed to discontinue the case, on 29.05.2018 Singapore confirmed the same, on 29.05.2018 the Court made an Order to discontinue the case based on the agreement of the Parties, of the proceedings instituted on 2.02.2017 and removed the case from the List,[42] thus the Court never had an opportunity to issue a decision on the application.

The Statute of the International Court of Justice provides for an additional set of conditions that are specific to this court. Indeed the Court may require previous compliance with the terms of the judgment before it admits proceedings in revision.[43] Further, the Statute makes a timeframe providing that the application for revision must be made at the latest within six months of the discovery of the new fact,[44] as no application for revision may be made after the lapse of ten years from the date of the judgment.[45]

1.3 In International Criminal Law

1.3.1 The Early Military Tribunals

On the one hand, the Statute of the International Military Tribunal of Nuremberg does not have a legal provision on the review process per se,

---

[40] Idem, para 28

[41] See Application for revision of the Judgment of 23 May 2008 in the case concerning sovereignty over Pedra/Pulau Batu Piteh, Middle Rocks and South Ledge (Malaysia/Singapore), 2017 General List No. 167, Letter from the Co-agent of the government of Malaysia to the Registrar of the International Court of Justice

[42] See Application for revision of the Judgment of 23 May 2008 in the case concerning sovereignty over Pedra/Pulau Batu Piteh, Middle Rocks and South Ledge (Malaysia/Singapore), Order of 29 May 2018

[43] Article 61(3)

[44] Article 61(4)

[45] Article 61(5)

however, it is interesting to note the wording of its article 29 according to which:

> [...]If the Control Council for Germany, after any Defendant has been convicted and sentenced, discovers fresh evidence which, in its opinion, would find a fresh charge against him, the Council shall report accordingly to the Committee established under Article 14 hereof for such action as they may consider proper, having regard to the interests of justice.

It will be recalled that the Control Council otherwise known as Amtsblatt des Kontrollrats in Deutschland was the executive authority of the Allied powers which controlled Germany in the aftermath of WWII. The above-cited article is the only article that refers to the possibility of finding new fact(s) otherwise termed as fresh evidence after the conviction and sentencing of the accused, although this provision suffers many critiques.

The law limits the actions of the Council only to a possibility where such evidence would lead to fresh charges, in which event the Council has to report to the Committee for further investigation and prosecution as determined by the law. The term Committee in this particular context could be understood as the prosecution. This law failed to provide for any course of action if the newly found evidence either by the Council, the Committee itself, or in casethe accused person would find fresh evidence not to establish new charges but rather to prove the accused innocence.

Having a legal provision on the possibility of finding fresh evidence leading to a new charge while not providing for a possibility of the opposite scenario would hardly be viewed to have met the principle of equality of arms as only one side of the proceeding has a possibility of bringing in new evidence but not the other.

Furthermore, it is noticeable that such fresh evidence is only brought in after the accused person has been convicted and sentenced, this locks out any new fact which could be brought in on a procedural order before the process had reached the conviction.

On the other hand, the Charter of the International Military Tribunal for the Far East of which article 17's chapeau reads "judgment and review" provides that:

> [...] Sentence will be carried out following the Order of the Supreme Commander for the Allied Powers, who may at

> any time reduce or otherwise alter the sentence, except to increase its severity.

This provision which rather draws its content from Article 29 of the Charter of the International Military Tribunal of Nuremberg which indicates that sentences shall be carried out following the orders of the Control Council for Germany, which may at any time reduce or otherwise alter the sentences, but may not increase the severity thereof…[46]

Such provisions are not to be understood as providing for any review process as discussed supra as they rather fall within the context of commuting the sentence. Indeed the powers to commute a sentence are powers given to the executive branch to reduce or rather lessen a sentence resulting from a criminal conviction. The decision to commute a sentence may be based on various factors including illness, age, expression of remorse and change of behavior, etc…

1.3.2 Ad Hoc Criminal Tribunals: The ICTY

According to Article 26 of the ICTY Statute:

> Where a new fact has been discovered which was not known at the time of the proceedings before the Trial Chambers or the Appeals Chamber and which could have been a decisive factor in reaching the decision, the convicted person or the Prosecutor may submit to the International Tribunal an application for review of the judgment.

This provision is further supplemented by Rule 119(A) of the Rules according to which:

> Where a new fact has been discovered which was not known to the moving party at the time of the proceedings before a Trial Chamber or the Appeals Chamber, and could not have been discovered through the exercise of due diligence, the defense or, within one year after the final judgment has been pronounced, the Prosecutor, may make a motion to that Chamber for review of the judgment. If, at the time of the request for review, any of the Judges who constituted the

---

[46] See Article 29 of the Charter of the International Military Tribunal of Nuremberg

original Chamber are no longer Judges of the Tribunal, the President shall appoint a Judge or Judges in their place.

1.3.2.1 The Dusco Tadic Case

On 5.10.2001, Dusco Tadic filed the Motion for Review before the President of the ICTY, seeking a review of his entire case on the ground that one of the Counsel of his defense team, acted against his interests while conducting investigations during the pre-trial and pre-appeal phases of his case. He submitted that in the Contempt Judgment, the Appeals Chamber found that his Counsel gave to the chief of the Prijedor Police Station, a list of potential witnesses who could have testified in Tadic's favor, despite knowing that this was against Tadic's interests as he was found guilty of various manipulations throughout the appeal preparations and the investigation conducted at that time to conceal the real perpetrators.[47]

The Defense submitted that the findings reached in the Contempt Judgment against one of the defense Counsels amounted to new facts not known to it at the relevant time. According to the Defense, until the Appeals Chamber had made its findings in the Contempt Judgment, Vujin's misconduct was not proven and not known to be true and, therefore, could not constitute a new fact, because it amounted to mere suspicion.[48]

In response to the Tadic Request for Review, the Prosecution submitted that the material contained in the application does not constitute new facts within the meaning of Rule 119 of the Rules. It stated that the disclosure of the witness list to Drljaca occurred before the start of the trial but was not brought to the attention of the Trial Chamber, notwithstanding that Tadic and his lead defense counsel, Wladimiroff, were aware of it.[49] The prosecution further submitted that none of the allegedly new facts could have amounted to a decisive factor in reaching the decision.[50]

Citing the Barayagwiza, Delic, and Jelistic cases the Tribunal said that for the deciding body to proceed to the review of its decision, the moving party must satisfy four preliminary criteria:

1. there must be a new fact;

47 ICTY, Prosecutor v. Dusko Tadic, Appeals Chamber, Decision on a motion for review,30.07.2002, para 6

48 Idem, para 8

49 Idem, para 12

50 Idem, para 15

2. that new fact must not have been known by the moving party at the time of the original proceedings;
3. the lack of discovery of the new fact must not have been through the lack of due diligence on the part of the moving party; and
4. the new fact could have been a decisive factor in reaching the original decision.

In its reasoning, the Court found that the first criterion requires the moving party to show the existence of a new fact.

Referring to the Jelisic case, the Tribunal said that a new fact may be defined as "new information of an evidentiary nature of a fact that was not in issue during the trial or appeal proceedings." Further, the Tribunal referred to the Delic case indicating that it is irrelevant whether the new fact already existed before the original proceedings or during such proceedings. What is relevant is whether the deciding body and the moving party knew about the fact or not.[51]

When assessing whether the fact of putting forward to the Appeals Chamber an Application case that was known to Vujin to be false would have been a decisive factor in reaching the verdict, the Tribunal noted that the finding that a false case was put forward in connection with Radic's statements could not assist the Applicant if his goal is to overturn the guilty findings concerning Omarska camp. The Tribunal reasoned that considering that the statements made by Radic did not form part of the evidence upon which the Appeals Chamber relied in convicting the Applicant. And further, the Tribunal found that it was unlikely that had the Appeals Chamber known of the falsity of the case presented by Vujin at an earlier stage, it would have considered this circumstance in favor of the Applicant. Thus the Tribunal concluded that the new facts were not to be considered a decisive factor within the meaning of Rule 120 of the Rules.[52]

The Tribunal went on to assess if the lack of knowledge of the new fact was due to the applicant's negligence. The Tribunal said that although it may not be excluded that Vujin told the Applicant about the falsity of the evidence proffered by Witness W, there was no evidence supporting such a hypothesis and thus it remained unlikely that the Applicant knew about it. Furthermore, it is unlikely that the Applicant could know about it using ordinary diligence

---

51 Idem, para 25

52 Idem, para 33

while being in detention in The Hague, far from the place where investigations conducted by Vujin were taking place.[53]

1.3.2.2 The Dario Kordic and Mario Cerkez Case

On 11.02.1999 the Appeals Chamber of the ICTY was seized by a request for review of a binding order of Trial Chamber III of 4 February 1999, filed by the Republic of Croatia. In the Binding Order, Trial Chamber III ordered the Requesting State to disclose certain documents to the Office of the Prosecution.

The Requesting State requests that the Appeals Chamber quash the Binding Order on the following two main grounds:

> 1) [T]he Binding Order was issued without the Requesting State having been given notice and an opportunity to be heard; and
> 2) The Binding Order is inconsistent with the criteria for the issuance of binding orders as established by the Appeals Chamber's Judgment on the Request of the Republic of Croatia for Review of the Decision of Trial Chamber II of 18 July 1997.[54]

One would notice that this request for review of an order of the Tribunal was instituted by the Republic of Croatia which was not a part of the criminal proceedings, and secondly, it was brought before the Appeals Chamber much that it rather had been issued by the Trial Chamber III. It is therefore filed under Rule 108 *bis* of the Rules according to which:

> A State directly affected by an interlocutory decision of a Trial Chamber may, within fifteen days from the date of the decision, file a request for review of the decision by the Appeals Chamber if that decision concerns issues of general importance relating to the powers of the Tribunal.[55]

Therefore this request for review falls outside the scope of this research as it is designed for a different and not based on the ground of discovery of new fact(s).

---

[53] Idem, para 35

[54] Appeals Chamber's Judgment on the Request of the Republic of Croatia for Review of the Decision of Trial Chamber II of 18 July 1997, page 2

[55] Rule 108(A) of the Rules

1.3.2.3 The Veselin Sljivancanin Case

On 28.01.2010 the Appeals Chamber of the International Tribunal for the Prosecution of Persons Responsible for Serious Violations of International Humanitarian Law Committed in the Territory of the former Yugoslavia since 1991 received an application of Mr. Veselin Sljivancanin who applied for the review of the Appeals Chamber judgment of 05.05.2009 on the ground of discovery of new facts with the context of Rule 119 of the Rules of Procedure and Evidence of the Tribunal hereinafter the Rules.[56]

It should be indicated that in this case the new facts were constituted by a statement of a witness namely Mr Panic, a Lieutenant-Colonel and Chief of Staff of the Guards Motorized Brigade "Gmtbr" and Operational Group South "OG South."[57]

The Tribunal indicated that a "new fact" within the meaning of Article 26 of the Statute and Rules 119 and 120 of the Rules consists of "new information of an evidentiary nature of a fact that was not in issue during the trial or appeal proceedings."[58] Further, citing its jurisprudence as well as the jurisprudence of the ICTR[59] the Tribunal indicated that under exceptional circumstances, the review may still be permitted even though the new fact was known to the moving party or was discoverable by it through the exercise of due diligence if a Chamber is presented with a new fact that is of such strength that it would affect the verdict and determines that review of its judgment is necessary because the impact of the new fact on the decision is such that to ignore it would lead to a miscarriage of justice.[60]

It is interesting to note that during the pleadings the discussion on the standard to be met for the Tribunal to put aside the four cumulative requirements namely

a) there is a new fact;
b) the new fact was not known to the moving party at the time of the original proceedings;

56 The decision concerning Veselin Sljivancanin's application for review, 14. 07. 2010 p 1

57 Prosecutor v. Veselin Sljiv Ancanin, Review Judgement, 8 December 2010, para 5

58 Decision with respect to Veselin Sljivancanin's application for review, 14. 07. 2010 p2

59 The Tribunal cited Tadic Decision, para. 27 (emphasis added). See also Rutaganda Decision, para. 8; Bla.fkic Decision, para. 8. BlaJkid Decision, para. 8 (citation omitted). See also Naletilic' Decision, para. 10; Rutaganda Decision, para. 8; Jean Bosco Barayagwiza v. The Prosecutor, Case No. ICTR-97-19-AR72, Decision (Prosecutor's Request for Review or Reconsideration), 31 March 2000 ("Barayagwiza Decision"), paras 63-69

60 Idem

c) the failure to discover the new fact was not due to a lack of due diligence on the part of the moving party; and
d) the new fact could have been a decisive factor in reaching the original decision, and granting the review based on the first two was not discussed.

The Tribunal simply restated that the impact of the Panic new fact, [...], is such that to ignore it would lead to a miscarriage of justice[61] and vacated the Appeals Chamber's previous judgment. An informed conclusion would require a full scale study of the case, however there is a danger when the judge assesses that they could decide on the application or non-application of the law as this behavior present a danger to the predictability of the law.

[61] Prosecutor v. Veselin Sljivancanin, Review Judgement, 8 December 2010, para 32

CHAPTER 2
THE BARAYAGWIZA CASE

On 1.12.1999 the prosecutor filed a motion for review or reconsideration of the Appeals Chamber's decision of 3.11.1999 in Barayagwiza's case. Indeed in its decision of 3.11.1999, the Appeals Chamber had found that the rights of the Appellant were repeatedly violated and that it appeared that the Prosecutor's failure to prosecute the case was tantamount to negligence. The Tribunal then concluded that the only remedy available for such prosecutorial inaction and the resultant denial of the Appellant's rights is to release the Appellant and dismiss the charges against him.[62] Further, the Tribunal found that the dismissal and release must be with prejudice to the Prosecutor stating that to proceed with the Appellant's trial when such violations have been committed would cause irreparable damage to the integrity of the judicial process.[63]

2.1 Applicable Rules

Article 25 of the Statute which provides for review proceedings stipulates that:

> Where a new fact has been discovered which was not known at the time of the proceedings before the Trial Chambers or the Appeals Chamber and which could have been a decisive factor in reaching the decision, the convicted person or the Prosecutor may submit to the International Tribunal for Rwanda an application for review of the judgment.

Rule 120 of the Rules provides for the request for review, accordingly:

> (A) Where a new fact has been discovered which was not known to the moving party at the time of the proceedings before a Trial Chamber or the Appeals Chamber and could

[62] ICTR, Prosecutor v. Jean Bosco Barayagwiza, Decision of 3.11.1999, para 106
[63] Idem, para 108

> not have been discovered through the exercise of due diligence, the Defense or, within one year after the final judgment has been pronounced, the Prosecutor, may make a motion to that Chamber for review of the judgment. If, at the time of the request for review, any of the Judges who constituted the original Chamber are no longer Judges of the Tribunal, the President shall appoint a Judge or Judges in their place.
> (B) Any brief in response to a request for review shall be filed within forty days of the filing of the request.
> (C) Any brief in reply shall be filed within fifteen days after the filing of the response.

Rule 121 of Rules which provides for preliminary examination stipulates that:

> If the Chamber constituted according to Rule 120 agrees that the new fact, if it had been proven, could have been a decisive factor in reaching a decision, the Chamber shall review the judgment, and pronounce a further judgment after hearing the parties.

2.2 The Admissibility of the Application

Before the Tribunal decided on the merit of the matter, the Tribunal saw it proper to address the question of admissibility of the application for review and reconsideration. Indeed after having been notified of the motion of the Prosecutor to review the Tribunal's decision, the Appellant filed four motions challenging the jurisdiction of the Appeals Chamber to entertain such application amongst other things, referring to the wording of the above-cited prescription, the Applicant submitted that Article 25 was only available to the parties after the accused had become a convicted person.[64]

This motion raises the question of whether the review process is understood to apply only after the final judgment has been issued and the procedure of appeals had been exhausted or whether it can also be referred to against any other order or decision of the tribunal in the same conditions, that is if the applicant had already referred to the appeals mechanism available to them.

---

64 ICTR, Prosecutor v. Jean Bosco Barayagwiza, Decision on the Prosecutor's request for review or reconsideration, 31.03.2000, para 27

Much that the reading of the article refers to the expression "convicted person," a literal interpretation of the text would tend to imply that before the accused is convicted this provision cannot be brought into application. However such restrictive interpretation seems not to hold water. The procedure of review is rather designed to be a mechanism through which any matter which has been decided in the final way by the tribunal in the sense that after the decision any unsatisfied party is given another opportunity to have the tribunal reopens under the conditions given by the law.

Thus, at any given point in time that any matter will have been decided by the appeals chamber would it be at the end of the proceedings or otherwise, would the tribunal had convicted or acquitted the accused, the law allows the parties to the proceedings to apply for a review if needed and if the requirements for the process are met.

It would be inconsistent to interpret Article 25 differently considering that the Appellant himself had earlier applied for revision much that he later withdrew his application when the Prosecutor responded requesting to be heard on the same. Indeed the Tribunal concluded that it was of the view that the intention of the legislation was not to interpret the Rules restrictively as suggested by the Appellant[65] as such; the review can be entertained even in cases of any other order or decisions including interlocutory motions.

2.3 The New Facts Standard

2.3.1 The Right to be Promptly Charged

In its decision of 3.11.1999, the Appeals Chambers found that:

> In the present case, the Appellant was detained for a total period of eleven months before he was informed of the general nature of the charges that the Prosecutor was pursuing against him. While we acknowledge that only 35 days out of the eleven months total are attributable to the Tribunal [...] the fact remains that the Appellant spent an inordinate amount of time in provisional detention without knowledge of the general nature of the charges against him regardless of which other parties may be responsible the

65 ICTR, Prosecutor v. Jean Bosco Barayagwiza, Decision on the Prosecutor's request for review or reconsideration, 31.03.2000, para 47

> inescapable conclusion is that the Appellant's rights to be promptly informed of the charges against him was violated.[66]

Thus the Appeals Chamber further found that the appellant's right to be promptly charged according to international standards as reflected in Rule 40bis was violated.[67]

Without submitting any evidence of notification of the charges to the Appellant, the Prosecutor submitted the transcript of 03.05.1996 of the Cameroonian Court according to which the Appellant addressed the Court and opposed Rwanda's request for extradition, stating that, "c'est le tribunal international qui est compétent."

Subsequently, the Appeals Chamber in its decision of 31.03.2000 on the review found that "it may accordingly be presumed that the Appellant was informed of the nature of the crimes he was wanted for by the Prosecutor"[68] and the Chamber considered this a new fact.

The Chamber reasoned that:

> [T]he Decision was based on the fact that: l'Appelant a été détenu pendant une durée totale de 11 mois avant d'être informé de la nature générale des chefs d'accusation que le Procureur avait retenus contre lui. The information now before the Chamber demonstrates that, on the contrary, the Appellant knew the general nature of the charges against him by 3 May 1996 at the latest. He thus spent at most 18 days in detention without being informed of the reasons therefor.[69]

The ground from which this decision is made is not solid, first one needs to keep in mind that the Chamber never had any evidence proving that the Appellant was ever notified of any charges against him, it assumed that if the Appellant stated that it is the international tribunal which has jurisdiction then he knew the charges against him.

If the Chamber wanted to reason by inference it should have satisfied itself that the only possible outcome of such inference is the conclusion it drew, however, this might not be necessarily the case. Indeed it turns out that during the proceedings before the Cameroonian Court, there was a debate

66 Idem, para 85
67 Idem, para 100
68 Idem, para 54
69 Idem

on the primacy of the international tribunal vis-à-vis domestic jurisdiction of which another transcript which would be submitted by the defense does not have the mention "c'est le tribunal international qui est compétent."

The contention on the authenticity of the transcript submitted by the Prosecutor will be discussed later suffice to indicate the assumption that because the Appellant simply stated that it is the international tribunal that is competent then he knew what were the crimes he was charged of seems weak, and further evidence would even weaken this assumption more.

Furthermore, it is of essence to note that on 16.05.1996 the Prosecutor had informed the Cameroonian authorities that she sought to transfer and hold in provisional detention under Rules 40bis four of the individuals who were co-detained by Cameroon but excluded the Appellant. Indeed on 15.10.1996, the Prosecutor wrote to the Appellant, indicating that Cameroon was not detaining him at her behest. As he was subsequently released considering that Cameroon rejected the application for extradition from Rwanda, nevertheless the Appellant was immediately re-arrested this time at the request of the ICTR Prosecutor. One cannot consider the information the Appellant had when he was arrested the first time as being valid when he was re-arrested the second time at the request of a different authority as these two proceedings are different.

In a nutshell, in the absence of an element of proof that the Appellant had been notified of charges against him, a notification which would allow him to prepare for his defense, the Chamber should not have considered the possibility that the Appellant was informed of charges brought before him as a new fact a conclusion arrived at as a matter of assumption.

2.3.2 The Willingness of the Republic of Cameroon

Whereas the decision of 03.11.1999 found that:

> There is no evidence here that either the Appellant sought to challenge his transfer to the Tribunal or that Cameroon was unwilling to transfer him on contrary the Deputy Prosecutor of the Cameroon Centre Province Court of Appeal appearing at the Rwanda extradition hearing on 31.05.1996 argued that the Tribunal had primacy and thus convinced that court to defer to the Tribunal. Moreover as noted above the President of Cameroon signed a decree order to transfer

> the Appellant before the signing of the Warrant of Arrest and Order for Surrender by Judge Aspergren on 23.10.1997 these facts indicate that Cameroon was willing to transfer the Appellant.[70]

In its Decision of 31.03.2000, the Chamber found that based on the evidence adduced at the time that "Cameroon was willing to transfer the Appellant", as there was no proof to the contrary. The Chamber further stated that the above information it has received shows that Cameroon had not been prepared to effect its transfer before 24.10.1997,[71] which the Chamber considered a new fact.

The Chamber arrived at that conclusion following the analysis of the report of Judge Mballe of the Supreme Court of Cameroon and the statement by David Scheffer, ambassador-at-large for war crimes issues, of the United States.

To start with, the report of Justice Mballe indicates that "if the legislative decree could be signed only on 21 October 1997 that was due to the pressure exerted by the Rwandan authorities on Cameroon for the extradition of detainees to Kigali." Although according to Ambassador Scheffer the signing of the Presidential legislative decree was delayed owing to the elections scheduled for October 1997.

Further, Mr. Scheffer states that he wrote to the Government of Cameroon on 13 September 1997 and that on or around 24 October 1997 the Cameroonian authorities notified the United States Embassy of their willingness to effect the transfer.

It is unclear how this information proves that the Cameroonian authorities were unwilling to effect the transfer indeed that the US Embassy made several representations to the Cameroonian authorities and when His Excellency Ambassador Scheffer wrote to the Cameroonian authorities they responded that they were willing to transfer the Appellant to the ICTR. One asks which element proves the unwillingness of such authorities to transfer the Appellant.

According to Justice Mballe it was due to the Government of Kigali which rather was pushing for the extradition of the Appellant to Kigali that the transfer to the Tribunal was executed. It is undeniable that the Rwandan

---

70 ICTR Prosecutor v. Jean Bosco Barayagwiza, Decision on the Prosecutor's request for review or reconsideration, 31.03.2000, para 59

71 Idem, para 57

Government had a particular interest in the case as it had requested the Appellant to be extradited to Kigali, this on its own does not prove beyond reasonable that there was no willingness of the Government of Cameroon to transfer the Appellant to the ICTR considering that the President of Cameroon had earlier signed a Decree order to transfer the Appellant before the signing of the Warrant of Arrest and Order for Surrender by the Hon. Judge Aspergren.

Considering that in its letter of on or about 24 October 1997 addressed to the US Embassy the Government of Cameroon indicated its intention to transfer the Appellant, coupled by the fact that it had earlier signed a Decree of transfer of the Appellant any conclusion on its unwillingness to transfer the Appellant is unsubstantiated. This does not deny the existence of foreign pressure to execute the same, however, concluding contrary to the conclusion of the Decision of 03.11.1999 could be overreaching particularly in the absence of any other evidence.

2.3.3 The Deferring of the Date of Initial Appearance

According to Article 19(3) of the Statute: "The Trial Chamber shall read the indictment, satisfy itself that the rights of the accused are respected, confirm that the accused understands the indictment, and instruct the accused to enter a plea. The Trial Chamber shall then set the date for trial." Further, rule 62 (A) of the Rules which provides for initial appearance stipulates that:

> Upon his transfer to the Tribunal, the accused shall be brought before a Trial Chamber or a Judge thereof without delay and shall be formally charged. The Trial Chamber or the Judge shall:
> (i) Satisfy itself or himself that the right of the accused to counsel is respected;
> (ii)Read or have the indictment read to the accused in a language he understands, and satisfy itself or himself that the accused understands the indictment;
> (iii) Call upon the accused to enter a plea of guilty or not guilty on each count; should the accused fail to do so, enter a plea of not guilty on his behalf;
> (iv)In case of a plea of not guilty, instruct the Registrar to set a date for trial;

According to the above provisions, the decision of 03.11.1999 Chamber indicated that the accused had to be brought before the assigned Trial Chamber and formally charged without delay upon transfer to the seat of the Tribunal.[72] The right of the accused as protected by these provisions is the right to appear before the Tribunal and be formally charged.

Interestingly in its decision of 31.03.2000, the Chamber noted amongst other items the letter indicating that the defense counsel entered into talks with the Registrar to set a date for the initial appearance. The Chamber found that the Registrar's letter indicating that Counsel assented to the initial appearance which was to place on 03.02.1997 was a new fact.[73]

The Chamber reasoned that the assent of the defense counsel to deferring the initial appearance until 03.02.1997 was a new fact for the Appeals Chamber as during the proceedings before the Chamber, only the judicial recess was offered by way of explanation for the 96-day period which elapsed between the Appellant's transfer and his initial appearance, and this was rejected by the Chamber. There was no suggestion whatsoever that the Appellant had assented to any part of that schedule.[74]

It emerges from the communication between the Defense Council and the Registry that there was a problem concerning the availability of judges and defense counsels. That the Defense Council after having been informed of such difficulties assented to the date of 03.02.1997 does not affect in any way the right of the Appellant to appear before the judge and be charged by the Tribunal.

Indeed it is at this juncture that one may refer to writ of habeas corpus as submitted by the Defense, unfortunately the writ was never responded to and no date was set for the Appellant to appear before the judge. Understood as a judicial remedy designed to protect a personal freedom or physical integrity against an arbitrary decision using a judicial decree ordering the appropriate authorities to bring the detained person before the judge so that the lawfulness of the detention may be determined,[75] it remains unclear why no action was taken to address various irregularities committed by various authorities in this case including the Tribunal itself as it missed the opportunity to respond the writ of habeas corpus.

---

72 Idem, para 70
73 Idem, para 60
74 Idem, para 61
75 Idem, para 88

Had the Tribunal availed itself to remedy the procedural misgivings which had already occurred at this stage, the outcome of the case could have been different, however, the Tribunal missed the opportunity and unfortunately, even the decision of the Chamber of 31.03.2000 remained silent on this pertinent aspect of the case.

It is a fact that the assent to the deferring of the initial appearance delays such appearances but the spirit of the law is to ensure that the right of the accused as far as the initial appearance is concerned is upheld as long as the accused has not appeared before the Tribunal his rights remains denied. If the exercise of the right is hindered by the holder of the right he loses the right to claim that his right has been denied which was not the case.

Considering the above discussion, the novelty of the letter of the Defense Counsel assenting to the date of 03.02.1997 as a new fact for review might be questionable in the sense that the right of the accused is to be brought before a judge until he appears before the Tribunal he has not benefited from such right and consequently, the finding of the Chamber of 03.11.1999 according to which: "There is no evidence that the Appellant was allowed to appear before an independent Judge during the period of the provisional detention and the Appellant contends that he was denied this opportunity"[76] cannot be unchallenged.

2.3.4 Unknown Fact to the Moving Party

In its discussion on whether the new facts were known to the moving party, in this case, the Prosecutor, the Chamber starts by indicating that: "Rule 120 introduces a condition which is not stated in Article 25 of the Statute which addresses motions for review."[77] Further, the Chamber found that: "The new facts identified in the first two periods were not known to the Chamber at the time of its Decision but they may have been known to the Prosecutor or at least they could have been discovered."[78]

In its reasoning, the Chamber would indicate that:

> In the wholly exceptional circumstances of this case, and in the face of a possible miscarriage of justice, the Chamber construes the condition laid down in Rule 120, that the fact be

---

76 Idem, para 61

77 Idem, para 63

78 Idem, para 64

> unknown to the moving party at the time of the proceedings before a Chamber, and not discoverable through the exercise of due diligence, as the directory in nature.[79]

Further, the decision indicates that the Chamber adopted such a position, considering that the Statute itself does not speak to this issue, which raises the question about the legal status of the Rules.

2.4 The Legal Status of the Rules of Procedure and Evidence

It needs to be pointed out that the Rules were adopted by the Tribunal under Article 14 of the Statute according to which:

> The Judges of the International Tribunal for Rwanda shall adopt, for proceedings before the International Tribunal for Rwanda, the Rules of Procedure and Evidence for the conduct of the pre-trial phase of the proceedings, trials, and appeals, the admission of evidence, the protection of victims and witnesses and other appropriate matters of the International Tribunal for the former Yugoslavia with such changes as they deem necessary.

Indeed such practice is well established in international law, save for the International Criminal Court whose Rules were adopted by States parties other major international courts and tribunals have had their rules of procedure adopted by the concerned tribunal itself that is they are adopted by a plenary session of all judges and are considered as part of the laws of the concerned court.

In practice, such rules are designed to flesh out the Statute which in most cases addresses mainly the substantive part of the law leaving the procedural rules to be addressed by the Rules of the Tribunal. Thus they are always read in conjunction with the Statute and they are carefully written n0t to conflict with the Statute in which case primary consideration will be given to the Statute, as by their nature the rules supplement the Statute which cannot address all procedural aspect of the proceedings.

As for their legal status, no international rule nor international court decision, or even any doctrine has ever challenged the legal nature of the Rules

---

[79] Idem, para 65

of any other international court, until the decision currently under study. The rules of procedure and evidence are binding in nature and cannot be considered as non-binding directive for which the Tribunal has the discretion to apply or not. To put it differently, there is no rule in international law which has ever questioned the binding nature of such Rules not in treaty law, and until the decision currently under study there had never been any jurisprudence which ever questioned the binding nature of the Rules as there is no doctrine in support of the reasoning of this judgment.

It is questionable for the Chamber to state that it has reached such a conclusion considering that the Rules address an issue that is not addressed by the Statute. One wonders whether the Rules should rather be designed to rephrase what has been stated in the Statute for their validity lest they become non-binding but would such reasoning not defeat the very purpose of the Rules? Indeed such rules are rather helpful when they address an issue for which no legal provision can be found in the Statute.

In addition, the Chamber's reference to exceptional circumstances of the case seems rather to be contrary to the doctrine of presumption of innocence. The Chamber never elaborated further on how the application of its rules would result in a miscarriage of justice. If this would have been the case the plenary session of the Tribunal should have amended the said Rules as it enacted them. However until they are duly amended they remain in application. Further it is equally questionable if the Appellant was not presumed innocent until proven guilty?

Discussing various techniques of interpretation of laws, Antonin Scalia and Brian Garner have stressed that the rule of interpretation according to which *verba cum effectu sunt accipienda*, that is, when interpreting a legal provision every word and every provision is to be given effect.[80] This means that no wording of the law should be ignored or no word of the law should be considered of no consequence as no word of the law cannot be meaningless as else they wouldn't have been made part of the law.

The technique of interpretation goes further suggesting that even in cases where a legal provision seems to create a *casus male inclusus* that is, in a case wrongly included the court should still give it an effect but it is not the function of the court to revise the law by subtraction.

---

[80] Antonin Scalia and Bryan A. Garner, Reading Law, The Interpretation of Legal Texts, Thomson/West, 2012, p150

Indeed emphasizing the same, Chief Justice John Marshall states:

> It would be dangerous in the extreme, to infer from extrinsic circumstances, that a case for which the words of an instrument expressly provide, shall be exempted from its operation.[81]

This is so because the choice given to the preference of a given word by the legislator implies that they intended that every word should be given a binding effect.

This understanding seems to be shared by Thomas M. Cooley according to whom "[T]he courts must . . . lean in favor of a construction which will render every word operative, rather than one which may make some idle and nugatory."[82] This statement seems valid not only for legal texts but even for any other writing: "Whenever a reading arbitrarily ignores linguistic components or inadequately accounts for them, the reading may be presumed improbable."[83] It then could be concluded as stated in Kungys v. United States, that it is a cardinal rule of statutory interpretation that no provision should be construed to be entirely redundant.[84]

Nevertheless in its conclusion the Appeals Chamber in its decision of 31.03.2000 agreed that the rights of the Appellant were violated and that all violations demand a remedy however it considered that since the violations he had suffered and the omissions of the Prosecutor were not the same as those which emerged from the facts on which the decision of 03.11.1999 was founded as the Chamber then quashed it early decision.[85]

Interestingly in its disposition, the Chamber altered the remedy provided in the decision of 03.11.1999 and rather provided for financial compensation for the Appellant if acquitted and a reduction of the sentence if found guilty.[86] It is questionable why would the Appeals Chamber consider financial compensation as such a remedy cannot be offered by the Tribunal as it lacks legal ground.

---

81 Sturges v. Crowninshield, 17 U.S. (4 Wheat.) 122, 202 (1819) (per Marshall, C.J.). See Ernst Freund, Interpretation of Statutes, 65 U. Pa. L. Rev. 207, 218 (1917)

82 Thomas M. Cooley, A Treatise on the Constitutional Limitations Which Rest upon the Legislative Power of the States of the American Union 58 (1868), as cited by Antonin Scalia and Bryan A. Garner, Reading Law, The Interpretation of Legal Texts, Thomson/West, 2012, p150

83 E.D. Hirsch, Validity in Interpretation 236 (1967)

84 *Kungys v. United States*, 485 U.S. 759, 778 (1988)

85 ICTR Prosecutor v. Jean Bosco Barayagwiza, Decision on the Prosecutor's request for review or reconsideration, 31.03.2000, para 74

86 Idem, para 75

2.5 The Defense Motion for Revision and /or Reconsideration

On 28.07.2000 the Defense filed a motion for revision and/or reconsideration of the Decision of 31.03.200 related to the revision of the Decision of 03.11.1999 and for stay of execution.

Considering that the Appellant's trial had been set for merit to be heard on 18.09.200 following the joinder of the indictment against the Appellant with those against Ferdinand Nahimana and Hassan Ngeze for a joint trial, amongst other things the Defense prayed the Appeals Chamber to order that execution of Chamber's Decision of 31.03.200 is stayed and consequently to order a stay proceedings before Trial Chamber I.

The Defense equally prayed the Appeals Chamber to invite or grant leave to the State of Cameroon to appear before the Appeals Chamber as amicus curiae and submit to the Chamber as soon as possible a report on the reasons for the length of time which elapsed between the 21.02.1997 Decision of the Yaounde Court of Appeal and 19.11.1997 the date on which the Appellant was transferred to the ICTR detention facility in Arusha and on any other matter specified by the Appeals Chamber.

Further, the Defense prayed the Appeal Chamber to invite the State of Cameroon to produce in *toto* and extensor all documents and correspondence of any kind without restriction which relate to the files concerning or touching on the case of the Appellant and of the 12 Rwandans of which he was one of them, whether the said documents and correspondence were part of the said files or not and whether they were treated as confidential or not.[87]

The Appellant submitted that such motion was submitted on the ground that he has discovered new facts of which both he and the Chamber were unaware at the time of the proceedings before the latter and which could have decisively affected the Decision the Appeals Chamber delivered on 31.03.2000 when it sat to review and/or reconsider the decision it delivered on 03.11.1999.[88]

The Defense would submit that the transcript alleged to be of 03.05.1996 proceedings as submitted by the Prosecution was false and inaccurate. The Defense rather produced what it claimed to be an authenticated copy of the Court record relating to the hearing of 03.05.1996.[89]

---

[87] See Extremely urgent motion by the Appellant for review and/or reconsideration of the Appeals Chamber Decision of 31.03.2000 and motion for stay of execution and of proceedings, para 2

[88] Idem, para 3

[89] Idem, para 5

Perhaps the most striking observation would be the submission that in reading the extract and the original of the notes permanently held at the Registrar's office of the Yaounde Court of Appeal the words "c'est le tribunal international qui est competent" do not appear and were never spoken by the Appellant.

This is striking because as indicated earlier in the Decision of 31.03.2000 the Chamber has indicated that:

> The Appellant addressed the court and opposed Rwanda's request for extradition, stating that, "c'est le tribunal international qui est compétent." The Appeals Chamber considers that it may accordingly be presumed that the Appellant was informed of the nature of the crimes he was wanted for by the Prosecutor. This was a new fact for the Appeals Chamber.[90]

Rather according to the records submitted by the Defense, the transcript reads "ça concerne le tribunal pénal international."[91]

Further, the defense submitted that the case file shows that the Court of Appeal in Cameroon held the Appellant awaiting the Prosecutor's file on the Appellant which was never communicated before the filing on 22.10.1997.[92] If this would have been verified by the Tribunal, any allegations on the unwillingness of the Cameroonian authorities would have been proven wrong. However as the Chamber declined to address the substance of the motion a position hardly understandable, the Tribunal missed the opportunity to address some of the key aspects of the case as it will be discussed later.

2.6 Motion for Revision or a Motion for Reconsideration

In response to the Appellant's motion, the prosecution raised the question that the motion did not clarify whether it was a motion for review or a motion for reconsideration.

As earlier indicated whereas the review process is founded upon the discovery of new facts, reconsideration is rather a process availed to any party

---

90 See ICTR Prosecutor v. Jean Bosco Barayagwiza, Decision on the Prosecutor's request for review or reconsideration, 31.03.2000, para 54

91 See Extremely urgent motion by the Appellant for review and/or reconsideration of the Appeals Chamber Decision of 31.03.2000 and motion for stay of execution and of proceedings, para 6-7

92 Idem, para 10

to request the chamber which decided on the matter to reopen the case based on the ground that the impugned decision was manifestly founded on an error which might cause injustice to the concerned party.

It should be indicated that the Statutes and Rules of the ad-hoc tribunals do not have a specific provision for this process. However, the jurisprudence of both the ICTR and ITCY seems to have settled the matter as it has consistently stated that:

> [A] Chamber has inherent discretionary power to reconsider a previous interlocutory decision in exceptional cases 'if a clear error of reasoning has been demonstrated or if it is necessary to do so to prevent injustice.[93]

A quick review of various applications for review/consideration submitted would appear rather to be an application for review as they have mostly limited themselves in demonstrating the existence of new facts without demonstrating why the application could be considered for reconsideration.

Indeed when applying for reconsideration, the moving party must demonstrate the existence of an error, and considering that this is not a usual process such party must further explain the particularity of the case which warrant the extraordinary process of reconsideration and demonstrate how this must be done to prevent an injustice.

Much that no legal definition of the concept of error is given in this particular situation, in the case of Slobodan Milosevic, the Tribunal highlighted that the concept could be could apply when there is a discernable error resulting in prejudice to a party based on an incorrect interpretation of law or based on the patently incorrect conclusion of facts unfair on unreasonable as to constitute an abuse of the Chamber's discretion or when the Chamber has given weight to extraneous or irrelevant consideration or that it has failed to give weight or sufficient weight to relevant consideration.[94]

Other than noting that the power to reconsider a previous decision remains a discretion of the concerned Chamber, a different element consists of a possible separation of the concept of error from the possible result of an injustice that is not necessarily caused by an error. This position seems to be consistent with the fact that for instance, a decision on the grant or refusal of

---

93 Prosecutor v. Radovan Kazadzic, Decision on judicial notice of the adjudicated fact, 4.05.2012

94 Prosecutor v Slobodan Milosevic, Confidential decision on the request of Serbia and Montenegro for review of the trial chamber's decision of 06 December 2005 para 16

extension on a given timeline might not necessarily be based on an error but is capable of causing injustices.

It thus can be concluded that a given Chamber has the inherent power to reconsider its own decisions and that it may grant a request for reconsideration if the moving party satisfies the Chamber of the existence of a clear error or that particular circumstances justify its reconsideration to avoid an injustice.[95]

Much that Judge Shahabudeen in his separate opinion state that such a possibility is designed to cure procedural irregularity that has caused a failure of natural justice,[96] it has not yet been settled definitively that there cannot be a request for reconsideration on substantive grounds.

2.7 The 14.09.2000 Decision

In her argument, the Prosecutor would reject allegations that the transcript that the prosecution filed earlier was not authentic stating that it would appear that both parties have a transcript relating to the same hearing both authenticated by competent Cameroonian court officials.[97] The prosecutor can only assume that one (or perhaps both) extracts of the transcript contain errors but it is impossible to say which one is more accurate.[98]

As the Appeals Chamber dismissed the motion the Chamber did not discuss the merit of the matter. Indeed the Chamber after having recalled that the Appeals' Chamber position in the 31.03.2000 decision in which it considered only a final judgment and that a final judgment is a decision which puts an end to the proceedings.[99] In the cited Decision the Chamber had pointed out that a final judgment in the sense of the Article 35 of the Statute and rule 120 of the Rules terminate the proceedings and only such a decision may be subject to review.[100]

---

95 See Prosecutor v. JadrankoPRLIC BrunoSTOJIC SlobodanPRALJAK MilivojPETKOVIC ValentinCORIC Berislav Pusic, Decision on Praljak Defence request for reconsideration or for certification to appeal the order of 14. 10. 2008 p4

96 Separate opinion Judge Shahabudeen, para 4

97 See Prosecutor's response to the extremely urgent motion by the Appellant for review and/or reconsideration of the Appeals Chamber Decision of 31.03.2000 and motion for stay of execution and of proceedings, para 35

98 Idem, para 36

99 ICTR Appeals Chamber Decision on review and/or reconsideration, 14.09.2000, p 3

100 ICTR Prosecutor v. Jean Bosco Barayagwiza, Decision on the Prosecutor's request for review or reconsideration, 31.03.2000, para 49

The 14.09.2000 decision reasoning would be that the 31.03.2000 is not a final decision:

> Considering the Review Decision the review which is requested did not put an end to the proceedings against the Applicant and in particular that the trial on merit is already on the Tribunal's schedule.

This raises several issues. To start with, it will be recalled that it is rather the Applicant who had brought the issue of inadmissibility of the motion for review submitted by the prosecution claiming that such remedy is only available at the end of the proceeding when the court has already convicted the accused person. In response, the Prosecution submitted that: "if a decision could be reviewed only following a conviction no injustice stemming from an unwarranted acquittal could ever be redressed."[101]

The chamber subscribed to the Prosecutor's reasoning that: "The wording of the article indicates that each of the parties may seek review of a decision, not that the provision is to apply only after a conviction has been delivered."[102] The Chamber then explained further that only a final judgment may be reviewed but this cannot be understood as to mean that it is at the end of the proceedings which is indeed the opposite of what the decision meant. This reasoning might exclude the use of this remedy to interlocutory motion as they usually happen before the case is decided on merit.

As already discussed one might rather conclude in the opposite direction indicating that the final nature of the decision should be understood to include any matter decided by the last resort for which no other "*recours*" can be done particularly when the procedure of appeal has been exhausted.

Secondly, the 14.09.2000 decision refers to the proceeding on merit which was scheduled to take place before the Trial Chamber. Perhaps this is even much weaker reasoning as one would ask under which circumstances could a decision of the Appeals Chamber be re-discussed by the Trial Chamber, indeed the matter was raised by the Appellant before the Trial Chamber during the closing hearing however the Trial Chamber rightfully declined to consider the motion.[103] The Chamber declared itself incompetent to deal with a question linked to a case under consideration by the Appeals Chamber.[104]

---

101 Idem, para 46

102 Idem, para 48

103 See Closing Hearing, Transcript of 11.09.2000

104 See Urgent motion requesting Examination of the Defense Motion dated of 28th July 2000, and Remedy for Abuse of Process,23.09.2005, para 1

Unless the reasoning of the Chamber means that the matter can always be revised when the Appellant appeal before the Appeals Chamber at the end of the proceedings which is counterproductive as it again defeats the meaning of interlocutory motion particularly if one considers the procedural aspect of such motions.

In the end, the Chamber discusses the availability of use of its power of reconsideration. The Chamber concludes that such power may not be used as a power of review in a situation in which review is not available. The statement of the Chamber seems confusing in the sense that if the Chamber understands that the procedure of review is referred upon discovery of new facts which were not known by the moving party but which could have influenced the outcome of the decision of the chamber and in this particular case the submission that the Prosecutor submitted a document of which authenticity is challengeable, the Chamber should find out if when the Tribunal decided on 31.03.2000 it knew that the said transcript was doubtful and what could be the impact of such new fact as this element- if proven- meet the threshold of being considered as a new fact.

Thus reasoning that the power of reconsideration may not be used as the power of review where the review is not[105] is hard to reconcile with the concept of reconsideration. Indeed it is my submission that the reconsideration procedure which is based on the existence of an error that causes injustice can be available where the review procedure is not. The two procedures can be triggered jointly as they can be triggered independently. If a motion for review is granted and the concerned chamber reopens the case there might not be necessarily a need of reopening the same case on the ground of reconsideration. As a matter of law, conditioning reconsideration to the existence of review is a reasoning which cannot be supported by any law or any other Court.

Furthermore, considering that the power of reconsideration is being exercised at the discretion of the Chamber at least within the context of the ICTR the three pages decision should have withheld to exercise such power rather on the ground of its discretion and this could have gone without any critique, however, the Chamber regrettably opted the other way round.

105 ICTR Appeals Chamber, Decision od review and/or reconsideration, 14.09.2000, p 3

2.8 The 23.06.2006 Decision on 23.09.2005 Motion

On 23.09.2005 the Defense filed an urgent motion requesting examination of the defense motion dated 28th July 2000 and remedy for abuse of process. In its introduction, the motion indicated that by its decision of 14.09.2000, the Appeals Chamber dismissed its motion of 28.07.2000 and referred it to the Trial Chamber however the Trial Chamber declined to consider it. The Defense submitted that as the motion has not been examined in its merit the Appeals Chamber was now requested to consider the 28.07.2000 motion and scrutinize the impugned material relied on by the prosecution in its application for review and or reconsideration of the decision of 3.11.1999.[106]

In addition to this request the Defense indicated that there was new material which has emerged and the defense submitted that the Appellant's actual statement to the court on 3rd May 1996 was distorted. Referring to the submissions which were made before the Trial Chamber where the Defense indicated that:

> We have got a positive judgment before the Tribunal of First Instance of Cameroon relative to the fact that the Minutes which were filed by the Prosecutor at the time of his Motion for review before the Appeals Chamber have been recognized obviously as being erroneous.[107]

Though the question of the authenticity of the minutes submitted by the Prosecutor has been raised in the previous motion it would appear that the judgment is rather additional evidence on the same.

The motion further raises an aspect that was now being raised for the first time concerning the report which had been submitted by Judge Mballe. The defense questions the reliability of Judge Mballe saying that at the time he submitted his report, he had no authority to do so, as he was no longer Director at the Ministry of Justice. However, it remains silent if Judge Mballe had the authority to issue such a report at the moment events relevant to his report occurred.

---

106 Urgent motion requesting Examination of the Defense Motion dated of 28th July 2000, and Remedy for Abuse of Process,23.09.2005, para 2

107 Idem, para 14

According to the Defense, it had the opportunity to inspect the file and submit that it contained evidence contradicting Mballe's report. Questioning the probative value of the Mballe report the Defense indicated that such report did not have any attached document in support of its claims, however, one wonders why was this aspect of the matter not raised by the Defense during the proceedings which led to the 31.03.2000 decision?

The Defense submitted that the Chief Registrar at the Tribunal of First Instance of Buea had indicated that there is no record of authentication of the Mballe report. The Buea Registrar reported that:

> There is no official record of the document titled 'Report CG. Mballe' in the Registry of this Court. The said C G Mballe has never been before this court either on the 18th or 19th to file or has he on any other date been to Registry to depose to the said document or any other document about the matter mentioned therein.[108]

Referring to the Semanza case, the Defense questioned Judge Mballe reliability. Indeed in the Semanza case, The Tribunal of First Instance of Buea had considered as null void another "Mballe Report" subsequently the Appeals Chamber rejected Semanza's Motion for review on the ground that the review was requested based on documents obtained by fraudulent means.[109]

Another aspect of this motion deserves particular attention. Though raised under the heading "lack of impartiality," the Defense attacks the decision of 31.03.2000 saying it was based on an incorrect interpretation of article 25 of the Statute and Rule 120 of the Rules the decision amounted to a serious error and/or abuse of process.[110] The defense thus indicated that a court had inherent powers to depart from its previous decision it also had the duty to reconsider its decision if it appears that there has been a serious error that lead to a miscarriage of justice.[111]

Much that the Prosecutor would respond that the allegations do not constitute a new fact but rather a complaint about the Appeals Chamber's interpretation of the submissions counsel for the Appellant made during

108 Idem, para 24
109 Idem, para 23
110 Idem. para 26
111 Idem. para 37

the hearing before it on 22.02.2000. This is not a matter for review or reconsideration.[112] Indeed as discussed earlier, the jurisprudence has established that in case of an error that leads the Tribunal to an unjust decision the Tribunal can reconsider such decision.

However, in its decision of 23.06.2006, the Appeals Chamber dismissed the motion saying that the proper place for such requests would be in an appeal against the Judgment on the merits.[113] Surprisingly when the defense appealed the judgment of the Trial Chamber, the Appeals Chamber held that the question of Appellant Barayagwiza's arrest and indictment had been dealt with in the Decision of 3.11.1999, as amended by the Decision of 31.03.2000. Recalling that the Appeals Chamber had already dismissed Appellant Barayagwiza's submissions regarding the legality of the proceedings which followed the Decision of 3.11.1999 the Appeals Chamber concluded that the Appellant had failed to demonstrate that jurisdiction was lost because of abuse of process.[114]

The Appeals Chamber's conclusion is hard to reconcile with the procedural history of this case. A quick recap of the history of the case reveals that on 28.07.2000 the Defense filed a motion for revision and/or reconsideration of the Decision of 31.03.2000 related to revision of the Decision of 03.11.1999 and for stay of execution which was dismissed by the Appeals Chambers on 14.09.2000 referring the Defense to raise the matter when pleading the case on its merit which were scheduled to take place before the Trial Chamber, which would decline having competence over the matter as it had been handled by the Appeals Chamber.

On 23.09.2005 the Defense filed an urgent motion requesting examination of the defense motion dated 28th July 2000, and remedy for abuse of process however in its decision of 23.06.2006, the Appeals Chamber dismissed the motion saying that the proper place for such requests would be in an appeal against the Judgment on the merits.

---

112 Prosecutor's response to "Appellant Jean-Bosco Barayagwiza's Motion Requesting Examination of Defense Motion dated 28 July 2000 and Remedy for Abuse of Process of 6.10.2005 para 16

113 Decision on Appellant Jean-Bosco Barayagwiza's Motion Requesting Examination of Defense Motion dated 28 July 2000 and Remedy for Abuse of Process,23 June 2006, as amended by the Corrigendum to the Decision on Appellant Jean-Bosco Barayagwiza's Motion Requesting Examination of Defense Motion dated 28 July 2000 and Remedy for Abuse of Process, 28 June 2006

114 ICTR Prosecutor v. Jean Bosco Barayagwiza, Decision on the Prosecutor's request for review or reconsideration, 31.03.2000, para 92

For the Appeals Chamber to hold that the Defense has failed to demonstrate that jurisdiction was lost because of abuse of process knowing that indeed the matter has never been considered in its merit by the Tribunal would imply that the accused has been denied justice.

Unfortunately, one of the grounds that the Defense was putting forth includes allegations that the Tribunal has taken certain decisions based on falsified documents and in another instance that the Tribunal relied on materials submitted by individuals with questionable character.

The seriousness of such allegations is such that they could tint the image of the entire justice system including individuals involved if such malpractice is proven before a court of law, however as the Tribunal missed the opportunity to address the matter the allegations will remain to the discredit of the Tribunal.

On multiple occasions, the Defense complained over the pressure exerted by the Government of Rwanda on the Tribunal, in response the Tribunal has given more time explaining all the safeguarding measures put in place to ensure the independence of the judiciary from the recruitment of judges to how they discharge their duties. The Tribunal however failed to understand how this explanation is uncalled for only if Tribunal was acting independently and deciding without influence.

Judge Rafael Nieto-Navia in his declaration dedicated a dozen of pages insisting on the independence of the Tribunal, however, it remains a fact that as a result of the decision of 31.03.1999 the pressure from the Government of Rwanda on the Tribunal was real to the point that some officials of the Tribunal were not having their visa to travel to Rwanda something which would jeopardize the discharge of their duties. If the Tribunal was independent it would not need to proclaim its independence and if it is not the same proclamation serve no purpose.

After discussing the procedural aspect of Barayagwiza trial, this research intends to continue the discussion on particular crimes for which Mr. Barayagwiza was found guilty by the Trial Chamber namely according to the charges:

Count 1: Conspiracy to commit genocide
Count 2: Genocide
Count 4: Direct and public incitement to commit genocide
Count 5: Crimes against humanity (Extermination)
Count 7: Crimes against humanity (Persecution)

However considering that the crime of crimes against humanity has already been discussed in our previous research,[115] the next part of the discussion will be focused on three crimes namely the Crime of genocide, the crime of conspiracy to commit genocide, and the crime of direct and public incitement to commit genocide.

115 See Gracieux Mbuzukongira, Aiding and Abetting by Omission: Special Focus on Mode of Participation to the Crime of Extermination in the Rutaganira Case, Galda-Verlage, 2019

CHAPTER 3

THE CRIME OF GENOCIDE

3.1 Evolution of the Law

Despite having occurred many times in the history of humanity,[116] the concept of genocide was first used by the Polish lawyer Raphael Lemkin around 1944 who understood genocide as:

> A coordinated plan of different actions aiming at the destruction of essential foundations of the life of national groups to annihilate the groups themselves. The objective of such a plan would be the disintegration of the political and social institutions of culture, language, national feelings, religion, and economic existence of national groups and the destruction of personal security, liberty, health, dignity, and even the lives of the individuals belonging to such groups.[117]

As indicated in the Goran Jelisic case, the conceptualization of the crime of genocide could be considered as a reaction to the horrors committed by the Nazis during WWII, not a surprise that the Convention has become one of

---

116 See The Convention on the Prevention and Punishment of the Crime of Genocide as it recognizes in its preamble that "at all periods of history genocide has inflicted great losses on humanity." Indeed Kriangsak Kittichaisaree, refers to the destruction of Armenians by the Ottoman Empire in 1915'16 during WWI, the Holocaust of the Jews by Nazi Germany, and the killing of millions of Cambodians by the Khmer Rouge regime in Cambodia in the mid-1970s all these killings happened in the twentieth century. See Kriangsak Kittichaisaree, International criminal law, Oxford University Press, 2005, p 67

117 See Raphael Lemkin, Axis rule in Occupied Europe, Laws of occupation, Analysis of Government, Proposals for redress, Washington 1944, 79 as cited by Giovanni Carlo Bruno, Le crime de genocide dans la jurisprudence des tribunaux penaux internationaux pour l'ex-yougoslavie et pour le Rwanda, in Emanuala Fronza and Stefano Manacorda, La justice penale international dans les decisions des tribunaux adhoc, Etudes des law Clinic en droit penal international, Dalloz, 2003, p 95.

the most widely accepted international instruments thus its provisions falling under customary international law.[118]

Conversely, neither the International Military Tribunal of Nuremberg nor the International Military Tribunal for the Far East would explicitly mention the crime of genocide. Though as indicated by Antonio Cassese, it could rather be considered as a subcategory of the crimes against humanity,[119] according to which crimes against humanity are understood:

> [N]amely, murder, extermination, enslavement, deportation, and other inhumane acts committed against any civilian population, before or during the war, or persecution on political, racial or religious grounds in the execution of or in connection with any crime within the jurisdiction of the Tribunal, whether or not in violation of the domestic law of the country where perpetrated.[120]

However one might submit that irrespective of the similarities between the crime of genocide and crimes against humanity, considering the special features of the crime of genocide prosecuting one crime to the other might not be the ideal situation.

Referring to the International Court of Justice advisory opinion of 1951 the Chamber rightfully would conclude that the crime of genocide is of the level of *jus cogens* because of its extreme gravity. Indeed the ICJ had indicated that it is difficult to imagine a convention that might have such dual character namely on one hand to safeguard the very existence of certain human groups and on the other confirm and endorse the most elementary principles of morality.[121]

Already on 11.12.1946, the UNGA had adopted its first Resolution 96(I) on the crime of genocide according to which:

> Genocide is a denial of the right of existence of entire human groups, as homicide is the denial of the right to

---

118 See Goran Jelisic Trial Chamber Judgment of 11.12.1999 para 60, see Akayesu TC 02.09.98 para 495, as cited David Boyle, Genocide et crimes contre l'humanite: Convergences et Divergeances, in , in Emanuala Fronza and Stefano Manacorda, La justice penale international dans les decisions des tribunaux adhoc, Etudes des law Clinic en droit penal international, Dalloz, 2003, p 124

119 Antonio Cassese, International Criminal Law, Oxford University Press, 2003, p96

120 Article 6(c) of the Charter of the International Military Tribunal.

121 ICJ, Case of the Reservations to the Convention on the Prevention and Punishment of the Crime of Genocide, Rec. 1951, p. 23

> live of individual human beings; such denial of the right of existence shocks the conscience of mankind, results in great losses to humanity in the form of cultural and other contributions represented by these human groups, and is contrary to moral law and to the spirit and aims of the United Nations.

Further, the same resolution would affirm that genocide is recognized as a crime under international law for which the commission of which perpetrators -whether private individuals, public officials, or statesmen, and whether the crime is committed on religious, racial, political, or any other grounds -are punishable as it attracts individual criminal responsibility even when committed as part of state policy.

Thus the General Assembly requested the Economic and Social Council to undertake the necessary studies, to draw up a draft convention on the crime of genocide to be submitted to the next session of the General Assembly. Sure enough, on 9.12.1948 the UNGA adopted its resolution 260 A (III) which approved and proposed for signature and ratification or accession of the Convention on the Prevention and Punishment of the Crime of Genocide.

According to Article 2 of the Convention on the Prevention and Punishment of the Crime of Genocide:

> In the present Convention, genocide means any of the following acts committed with the intent to destroy, in whole or in part, a national, ethnical, racial, or religious group, as such:
>
> (a) Killing members of the group;
> (b) Causing serious bodily or mental harm to members of the group;
> (c) Deliberately inflicting on the group conditions of life calculated to bring about its physical destruction in whole or in part;
> (d) Imposing measures intended to prevent births within the group;
> (e) Forcibly transferring children of the group to another group.

It should be indicated that the same text has been coopted by the ICTR and the ICTY respectively in their articles 6 and 4. As said by Raphael Lemkin:

"Genocide is directed against the national group as an entity and the actions involved are directed against individuals not in their capacity, but as members of the national group."[122]

This position is well elaborated by Kittichaisaree: "The victim of the crime of genocide is the group itself and not the individual."[123] Indeed through the same lens, one can even submit that the victim of the crime of genocide is rather the entire mankind, in the sense that if genocide is carried out and an entire national group is decimated it is rather the entire mankind or the entire humanity which last one of its "layers" and becomes a victim for that. This would explain why the crime of genocide rightly referred to as crime of crimes creates obligations *erga omnes* that is an obligation that each State owes to the entire community of States.

3.2 Material Elements of the Crimes

The law provides for the facts which constitute the *actus reus* of the Crime of genocide as will be hereunder discussed.

3.2.1 Killing Members of the Group

It needs to be pointed out at the outset as indicated in the Akayesu case, the Chamber noted that the use of the 1948 convention against genocide and the ICTR Statute uses the term "*meurtre*" in the French version while the English version rather uses the term "killing". The Trial Chamber believes that the term "killing" used in the English version is too general since it could very well include both intentional and unintentional homicides, whereas the term "*meurtre*", used in the French version, is more precise.[124] Commenting on the Trial Chamber's judgment Professor Cassese indicates that the concept of killing must be interpreted as murder meaning voluntary or intentional killing.[125]

122 See Raphael Lemkin, Axis rule in Occupied Europe, Laws of occupation, Analysis of Government, Proposals for redress, Washington 1944, 79 as cited by Giovanni Carlo Bruno, Le crime de genocide dans la jurisprudence des tribunaux penaux internationaux pour l'ex-yougoslavie et pour le Rwanda, in Emanuala Fronza and Stefano Manacorda, La justice penale international dans les decisions des tribunaux adhoc, Etudes des law Clinic en droit penal international, Dalloz, 2003, p 95

123 See Kriangsak Kittichaisaree, International criminal law, Oxford University Press, 2005, p69

124 Prosecutor v. Jean-Paul Akayesu, Trial Chamber Judgment of 2.09.1998 para 500

125 Antonio Cassese, International criminal law, Oxford University Press, 2003 p 102

Referring to the *travaux préparatoires* of the Convention, the Chamber indicates that the proposal by certain delegations that premeditation be made a necessary condition for there to be genocide, was rejected because some delegates deemed it unnecessary for premeditation to be made a requirement as by its nature, the crime of genocide, necessarily entails the element of premeditation.[126]

However, in the Kayishema and Ruzindana case the Appeals Chamber held that it understood the Trial Chamber's reasoning to be that, if a doubt exists in the interpretation of a statute, the doubt must be interpreted in favor of the accused. The Trial Chamber considered that "*meurtre*" is not the same as "killing". However, having regard to the operative part of Article 2(2) of the Statute, it found that "there is virtually no difference" between the two terms as the term "killing" is linked to the intent to destroy in whole or in part.[127]

The Appeals Chamber concluded that it accepts this view, but stated that if the word "virtually" is interpreted in a manner that suggests a difference, though minimal, between the two terms, it would construe them both as referring to intentional but not necessarily premeditated murder, this being, in its view, the meaning to be assigned to the word "*meurtre*".[128]

It is noticeable that the wording of the convention deliberately uses the terminology killing of members of the group in the plural, thus Professor Cassess raising "another interesting problem relating to *actus reus* is whether genocide may also include the killing, of one single member of a protected group." This finds the answer in the Akayesu Judgment which indicates that: "the murder of a particular individual, for the realization of an ulterior motive, which is to destroy, in whole or part, the group of which the individual is just one element."[129] This can be understood as providing a positive answer to the question as indeed the killing of one person by a given accused person can still constitute if it is part of a widespread killing which qualifies for genocide.

3.2.2 Protected Groups

As far as membership of the protected group is concerned, the Convention specifically considers national, ethnic, racial, or religious groups as protected groups for protection against genocide.

---

126 Prosecutor v. Jean-Paul Akayesu, Trial Chamber Judgment of 2.09.1998 para 501

127 ICTR, Prosecutor v. Kayishema and Ruzindana, Appeals Chamber Judgement, 04.12.2001 para 151

128 Idem, para 151

129 Prosecutor v. Jean-Paul Akayesu, Trial Chamber Judgment of 2.09.1998 para 522

Much that in the Akayesu case, the Trial Chamber held that the crime of genocide was allegedly perceived as targeting only "stable" groups, constituted in a permanent fashion and membership of which is determined by birth. The Chamber would further conclude that a common criterion in the four types of groups protected by the Convention is that membership in such groups would seem to be normally not challengeable by its members, who belong to it automatically, by birth, in a continuous and often irremediable manner.[130] As said by Professor Schabas "On closer scrutiny, three of the four categories in the Convention enumeration, national groups, ethnic groups, and religious groups seem to be neither stable nor permanent."[131]

It thus becomes challenging to establish common criteria that the drafters of the Convention used to determine which group should be considered a protected group under the Convention particularly when the Convention itself does speak to that.

3.2.2.1 National Group

In the Akayesu case, citing the Nottebohm decision of the International Court of Justice, the Trial Chamber held that a national group is defined as a collection of people who are perceived to share a legal bond based on common citizenship, coupled with reciprocity of rights and duties.[132]

This definition however has been criticized that in the Nottebohm, the Court was interested in defining the meaning of "nationality" in the context of espousal as it had no interest in the meaning of "national group"[133] as a group. Indeed the determination of the citizenship of an individual might not necessarily coincide with the same determination once made in a context of a group, particularly in a situation where no formal State exists yet a particular group of people who for instance belong to a given territory which has not yet attained statehood and cannot be protected under the three other groups provided for by the Convention. Hence, Carol Lingaas caution not

---

130 The same having been referred to in the Jelesic Goran Case Trial Chamber Judgment para 69 see Prosecutor v. Jean-Paul Akayesu, Trial Chamber Judgment of 2.09.1998 para 511

131 William Schabas, Groups protected by the genocide convention: Conflicting interpretations from the international criminal tribunal for Rwanda, Journal of International & Comparative Law, Vol. 6, p 382

132 Prosecutor v. Jean-Paul Akayesu, Trial Chamber Judgment of 2.09.1998 para 512

133 David Lisson, Defining "national group" in the genocide convention: A case study for Timor-Leste, Stanford Law review, Vol 60, 2008, p 1468

to juxtapose the concept of nationality with the concept of citizen seems valid.[134]

Much that the adoption of the concept of the national group seems to have been easily accepted by the drafter of the Convention in practice it has proven difficult to draw consensus, particularly in the jurisprudence.[135]

3.2.2.2 Ethnic Group

The Akayesu Case indicates that an ethnic group is generally defined as a group whose members share a common language or culture.[136] The same was referred to by the UN Commission of Inquiry on Darfur as it indicates that an ethical group may be taken to refer to sets of individuals sharing a common language, as well as common traditions or cultural heritage.[137]

This definition however brings a series of challenges, particularly in the context of Rwanda where the various ethnic groups do share the language, culture, and tradition. Perhaps Tamotsu Shibutani definition might be more helpful in this regard as he understands the concept of an ethnic group as being composed of individuals who conceive themselves as being alike by their common ancestry, real or fictitious, and who are so regarded by others.[138] One may view two distinctive elements of self-identification of the members of the group but also the conception of the rest of the ethnic formations of the society.

Thus in the Kayishema and Ruzindana case, the Tribunal found that: "An ethnic group is one whose members share a common language and

---

[134] See Carola Lingaas Saying that in the Nottebohm case, the ICJ took an objective view of nationality that prevailed over the subjective views of the individual. By referring to Nottebohm, the ICTR juxtaposed nationality with citizenship. This approach is not uncontested. Indeed, there are discrepancies concerning the definition of a national group, which range from national minorities to citizenship and even to the homeland as a broader concept. See Carola Lingaas, Defining the protected groups of genocide through the case law of international courts, ICD Brief 18 December 2015, p 6

[135] See ICTR, Prosecutor v. Rutaganda, Trial Chamber Judgment, 6.12. 1999, para. 56: "[T]here are no generally and internationally accepted precise definitions [of] national, ethnical, racial and religious groups For further review on the jurisprudence see Agnieszka Szpak, National, Ethnic, Racial, and Religious Groups Protected against Genocide in the Jurisprudence of the ad hoc International Criminal Tribunals, The European Journal of International Law Vol. 23 no. 1, 2012

[136] Prosecutor v. Jean-Paul Akayesu, Trial Chamber Judgment of 2.09.1998, para 513

[137] Report of the International Commission of Inquiry on Darfur to the United Nations Secretary-General, UN Doc. S/2005/60, 25 January 2005, para. 494

[138] Tamotsu Shibutani and Kian Kwan, Ethnic Stratification: A Comparative Approach (New York: Macmillan Company, 1965), p. 42, as cited by Carola Lingaas, Defining the protected groups of genocide through the case law of international courts, ICD Brief 18 December 2015, p 7

culture; or, a group which distinguishes itself, as such (self-identification); or, a group identified as such by others, including perpetrators of the crimes (identification by other)."[139]

It then could be concluded that whereas there are objectives criteria that could be considered as a starting point, it remains important that a subjective element is coupled to such a definition. This was highlighted in the Rutaganda case indeed the Trial Chamber noted that to apply the Genocide Convention, membership of a group is, in essence, a subjective rather than an objective concept. The victim is perceived by the perpetrator of genocide as belonging to a group slated for destruction. In some instances, the victim may perceive themselves as belonging to the said group.[140]

In the Semanza case, the Trial Chamber held that "the determination of whether a group" can be defined as a target group "ought to be assessed ... by reference to the objective particulars of a given social or historical context, and by the subjective perceptions of the perpetrators."[141] Thus, in the Karemera case, the Appeals Chamber ruled authoritatively that Trial Chambers must take judicial notice of the fact that Hutu, Tutsi, and Twa are considered protected groups falling under the Genocide Convention.[142]

3.2.2.3 Racial Group

Whereas in the Akayesu case, the Tribunal stated that: "The conventional definition of a racial group is based on the hereditary physical traits often identified with a geographical region, irrespective of linguistic, cultural, national or religious factors."[143] Rather the 1950 UNESCO declaration on the race question defines the concept of race as one of the groups of populations constituting the species Homo sapiens. It indicates that as long as these populations are capable of inter-breeding with one another they then belong to the same race.[144]

The declaration further clarifies that "the term 'race' designates a group or population characterized by some concentrations, relative as to frequency

---

139 Prosecutor v. Clement Kayishema and Obed Ruzindana, Trial Chamber II, Judgment, 21 May 1999, para 98

140 Prosecutor v. Georges Anderson Nderubumwe Rutaganda, Trial Chamber I, Judgment and Sentence, 6. 12. 1999, para 56

141 ICTR, Prosecutor v. Semanza, Trial Chamber Judgment, para. 317

142 ICTR, Prosecutor v. Karemera Appeals Chamber Judgment, 16.06.2006, para. 25

143 ICTR, Prosecutor v. Akayesu Trial Chamber Judgment, para 514

144 See the 1950 UNESCO declaration on the race question, para 3

and distribution, of hereditary particles (genes) or physical characters, which appear, fluctuate, and often disappear over time because of geographic and/or cultural isolation."[145]

It thus clarifies that many national, religious, geographic, linguistic or cultural groups have, in such loose usage, been called 'race', accordingly it states that in reality people who live in Iceland or England or India are not races; nor are people who are culturally Turkish or Chinese or the like thereby describable as races.[146] Addressing a possible classification amongst the Homo-Sapiens the declaration indicates that most anthropologists agree on classifying the greater part of present-day mankind into three major divisions namely the Mongoloid, the Negroid, and Caucasoid. However, it further states that such division is rather dynamic, and not static.[147]

It would look obvious that the context in which the Convention was adopted might not have been understood the same as it is understood within the framework of the 1950 UNESCO Declaration on the question of race. Indeed the wrongly assigned meaning of racial division in the Convention is a reflection of the misconception of the concept at the time of its conception which might have been equally influenced by the various factors including the political factors which dominated the European view of the concept then. Such a viewpoint might have reduced the concept of race as low as to certain national groups, for instance considering a particular national group as a higher race when such group is not a racial group to start with.

How the concept of race could still be made useful will depend on other factors including the perception both of the protected and the criminal, not necessarily with the scientific definition of the concept but also it could be mirrored to the meaning assigned to other protected groups and the assessment must take into consideration the particularities of a given situation within a particular context. As said in the Bagilishema case, the Trial Chamber indicated that such particularities could include political, social, historical, and cultural contexts.[148]

---

145 Idem, para 4

146 Idem, para 5

147 Idem, para 7

148 See ICTR, Prosecutor v. Bagilishema, Trial Chamber Judgment, para 65

3.2.2.4 Religious Group

A religious group is one whose members share the same religion, denomination, or mode of worship.[149] Much that the Akayesu case stated that Article 2 of the Statute, should be limited to only the four groups expressly mentioned as it understood these groups as stable and permanent, for which one belong at birth,[150] none of these criteria applies to any of the four protected groups. Indeed there is no religion that one is bound to belong to permanently, the same being true for other groups.

Further, it could be noted that within in many cases, the way of worship can be intertwined with the cultural practices and beliefs of a given group thus linking together elements of religious, ethnic national, or even "racial" groups. Hence one might conclude with Professor Schabas words indicating that there is a danger that a search for autonomous meanings for each of the four terms will weaken the overarching sense of the enumeration as a whole. As he further says: "Deconstructing the enumeration risks distorting the sense that belongs to the four terms, taken as a whole."[151] Indeed the four terms in the Convention not only overlap, they also help to define each other.[152]

3.2.3 Causing Serious Bodily or Mental Harm to Members of the Group

No treaty has defined the concept of bodily and mental harm. Though, international jurisprudence has given enough guidance on the same. According to the International Law Commission, bodily or mental harm inflicted on members of a group must be of such a serious nature as to threaten its destruction in whole or in part.[153] Thus in the Kayishema and Ruzindana case, the Tribunal defines the concept of serious bodily harm as "harm that seriously injures the health, causes disfigurement or causes any serious injury to the external, internal organs or sense."[154]

---

149 See ICTR, Prosecutor v. Akayesu Trial Chamber Judgment, para 515

150 Idem, para 516

151 William Schabas, Groups protected by the genocide convention: Conflicting interpretations from the international criminal tribunal for Rwanda, Journal of International & Comparative Law, Vol. 6, p 386

152 Idem, p 385

153 Report of the International Law Commission on the work of its forty-eighth session, p 46 para(16)

154 See ICTR Prosecutor v. Clement Kayishema and Obed Ruzindana, Trial Chamber Judgement, para. 109

The tribunal further refers to the Akayesu case highlighting that acts of sexual violence, rape, mutilations, and interrogations combined with beatings, and/or threats of death, were all acts that amount to serious bodily harm.[155] However much that death threats rather still reach the threshold to be considered as causing mental harm rather than bodily harm. It needs to be pointed out that as indicated in the Akayesu case such serious bodily harm does not necessarily mean harm that is permanent or irremediable.[156]

As to serious mental harm, the Seromba case indicates that such harm includes threats that are of the intensity that causes more than minor or temporary impairment of mental faculties such as the infliction of strong fear or terror, intimidation or threat as long as the threat is of such a serious nature as to threaten its destruction in whole or in part.[157]

It is important to note that either for serious bodily or mental harm a determination needs to be made on a case-by-case basis, particularly so for mental harm which is a very subjective factor.

3.2.4 Inflicting Conditions Calculated to Destroy the Group

In the Akayesu case, the Tribunal held that the expression deliberately inflicting on the group conditions of life calculated to bring about its physical destruction in whole or in part, could be understood as any method of destruction by which the perpetrator does not immediately kill the members of the group, but which, ultimately, seek their physical destruction.[158] Further, the Tribunal found that for instance subjecting a group of people to a subsistence diet, systematic expulsion from homes, and the reduction of essential medical services below the minimum requirement.[159]

In the Kayishema and Ruzindana case, the Tribunal found that situations that are likely to cause death if left to run their course, irrespective of whether death occurs,[160] if a given circumstance will lead to a slow death for instance housing, clothing, hygiene and medical care or excessive work or physical exertion[161] such methods do not lead to death immediately but they surely lead to death including starvation.[162]

---

155 Idem, para 108
156 ICTR, Prosecutor v. Akayesu, Trial Chamber Judgement, para 502
157 ICTR, Prosecutor v. Seromba Trial Chamber Judgement, para 46
158 ICTR, Prosecutor v. Akayesu, Trial Chamber Judgement, para 505
159 Idem, para 506
160 ICTR. Prosecutor v. Kayishema and Ruzindana, Trial Chamber Judgment, para 114
161 Idem, para 115
162 Idem, para 116

It is important to note that the ultimate aim of the criminal act must be the death of the targeted group. Thus, in the Tolimir Zdravka case, the Appeals Chamber found that forcible transfer operations in Srebrenica and Zepa were not conducted under circumstances calculated to result in the total or partial physical destruction of the protected group. Indeed the Appeals Chamber reasoned that much that the Bosnian Muslims who were forced to abandon their houses and belongings in Srebrenica and Zepa endured a painful process of separation from their ancestral land and transferred to other parts of BiH were traumatized and faced harsh realities in their lives, both financially and psychologically, it has not been established beyond reasonable doubt that such a policy of removal was aimed at causing the physical destruction, i.e., the slow death, of these populations. Referring to the Trial Chamber findings according to which the transferred populations to ABiH-held territory were safe and did not run any risk of physical extinction.[163]

This reasoning was supported by ICJ ruling in Croatia v. Serbia case, as the Court said that to determine whether the forced displacements constitute genocide the Court will seek to ascertain whether those forced displacements took place in such circumstances that they were calculated to bring about the physical destruction of the group. As the Court further would indicate that the circumstances in which the forced displacements were carried out are critical in this regard.[164]

3.2.5 Imposing Measures Intended to Prevent Births

In the Akayesu case the Tribunal held that the measures intended to prevent births within a group should be construed as sexual mutilation, the practice of sterilization, forced birth control, separation of the sexes, and prohibition of marriages. It further states that the material element is satisfied in the case where a woman of the said group is deliberately impregnated by a man of another group, with the intent to have her give birth to a child who will consequently not belong to its mother's group, particularly in a patriarchal society.[165]

A typical example of measures intended to prevent births could be seen in the Eichmann Case where it was found that through the prevention of

[163] ICTY, Prosecutor v. Tolimir Zdravka, Appeals Chamber Judgment, para 233
[164] ICJ, Croatia v. Serbia, Judgment para 163
[165] ICTR, Prosecutor v. Akayesu Trial Chamber Judgment, para 507

births from the Kovno Ghetto and from Terezin. Germans published an order in July 1942 for the termination of all pregnancies except those in the eighth or ninth months. A woman whose pregnancy was not terminated despite the order was liable to the death penalty.[166]

Further, a statement dated 21 August 1843, sent by Dr. Munk, Director of the Health Services in the ghetto, to the Chief Medical Officer and all the gynecologists indicated that all fathers of children conceived here, and also the mothers and the children, will be included in transports and deported.[167]

In the Ulrich Gretfelt and others case the Decree of Himmler in 1943 indicated that in case of pregnancy of female workers if the man is of a foreign race that is understood as not of Germanic origin the pregnancy may be terminated or the child may be taken away. It further stated that no abortion could be performed where a child of good character might be expected and that an abortion should be performed where such a child was improbable. Indeed the desired result was to keep the Eastern workers mainly the Poles available as slaves but also to hamper the reproduction of the population of Eastern nations.[168]

Discussing the question of rape as part of measures intended to prevent births in the Akayesu case, the Tribunal noted that rape can be considered as a measure intended to prevent births when the person raped refuses subsequently to procreate, in the same way, that members of a group can be led, through threats or trauma, not to procreate.[169] This position however raises a question as to how could the criminal predict the behavior of her victim as a result of rape, as it is not established that the victim of such crime would ipso facto behave in a certain way.

Nevertheless, it needs to be indicated that even if a given measure does not prevent birth in totality even a partial prevention of reproduction is enough for the offender to be found guilty of genocide for having taken or implemented measures intended to prevent births.[170]

---

166 In the District Court of Jerusalem, Criminal Case No. 40/61, Adolf Eichmann, Judgment, 1968, para 159

167 Idem, para 159

168 Military Tribunal I, Transcript of Judgment and Sentence 1948, Trial 8

169 Idem, para 508

170 Machteld Boot, Genocide, Crimes against humanity and war crimes, 2002, para. 422

3.2.6 Forcibly transferring Children of the Group to Another Group

The term forcing transfer of children from one group to another would be better understood if one refers to the Ulrich Gretfelt v. USA. Indeed the 1939 Treatise on the problem of the manner of dealing with a population of the former Polish territories based on racial political aspects, for the Germanization of the Nordic groups directed amongst other things deportation of population and the resettlement of Germans.[171]

The treatise indicated that children not to be over 8 to 10 years of age because as a rule a genuine ethnic transformation that is a final Germanisation is possible only up to this age, are to be prevented with all connection with their Polish relative, give them Germans names, transfer them to German educational institutions. The treatise provided even for the kidnapping of children to train them in Nazi ideology.[172]

The ICC Element of Crimes has listed the following elements as constitutive of this crime namely:

- The perpetrator forcibly transferred one or more persons.
- Such person or persons belonged to a particular national, ethnic, racial, or religious group.
- The perpetrator intended to destroy, in whole or in part, that national, ethnic, racial, or religious group, as such.
- The transfer was from that group to another group.
- The person or persons were under the age of 18 years.
- The perpetrator knew or should have known, that the person or persons were under the age of 18 years.
- The conduct took place in the context of a manifest pattern of similar conduct directed against that group or was conduct that could itself affect such destruction.

Though discussed not as constitutive of the crime of genocide in the Blagoje Simic and others case the Trial Chamber II addressed the matter of

171 Military Tribunal I, Transcript of Judgment and Sentence 1948, 10 Mar 48-M-TE-3-1-Gaylord (Int. Treidell) Court I case 8 p 5288

172 Idem

deportation and unlawful or forcible transfer highlighting the involuntary and unlawful displacement, nature of the movement, or relocation, of persons from the territory in which they reside[173] to another place.

It should be indicated that since the provision applies to protect children against forceful transfer the concept is understood as applicable to children as defined by the CRC that is every human being below the age of eighteen years.[174] Furthermore considering that consent at this particular age is immaterial that means that even in the event the victim of the crime might have "consented" such consent remains immaterial to the commission of the crime. It should be indicated further that even when children are not mistreated during and after the transfer the crime remains the same. Indeed the crime aims at uprooting the victims from their cultural identity the fact that they were not mistreated is irrelevant to the commission of the crime, however, if in the process other crimes were committed including torture then and accused will face the additional charges accordingly.

3.3 The Intent to Destroy

One of the most distinctive features of the crime of genocide is the psychological element of this crime. This is viewed in the legal definition of the crime which clearly states that genocide means any of the prohibited acts committed with the intent to destroy. Such intent could be understood as a particular state of mind which aims at the result or the consequence of the prohibited act.[175]

Referring to the Krstic case, the ICJ held that it could be concluded that under the heading intent to destroy, the characterization of genocide encompasses acts committed to destroying all or part of a group.[176] The same ICJ decision indicates that:

> It is not enough to establish, for instance in terms of paragraph (*a*), that deliberate unlawful killings of members

[173] ICTY, Prosecutor v. Blagoje Simic, Miroslave Tadic, Siro Zaric, Judgment Trial Chamber II, 17.10.2003, para 121

[174] Article 1 UN Convention on the Rights of a Child

[175] ICTY, Prosecutor v Krstic, Trial Chamber Judgment, para 571

[176] International Court of Justice, Case concerning the application of the convention on the prevention punishment of the crime of genocide, (Bosnia and Herzegovina v. Serbia and Montenegro) Judgment of 26 February 2007, para, 292

> of the group have occurred. The additional intent must also be established and defined very precisely. It is often referred to as a special or specific intent or *dolus specialis*.[177]

The requirement that the commission of the crime of genocide is committed with a special intent can be explained by the place that the crime itself and the convention against genocide has in international law. Already the International Law Commission's work after having discussed the extreme gravity of the crime of genocide reminds us of how the convention was widely accepted by the international community by way of ratifying the convention overwhelmingly by the majority of States.[178]

Further the ICJ in its advisory opinion of 1951 raises a pertinent aspect that is the object of the convention itself being on the one hand to safeguard the very existence of certain human groups and on the other to confirm and endorse the most elementary principles of morality. It further indicates that in such a convention the contracting States do not have any interests of their own; they merely have, one and all, a common interest, namely, the accomplishment of those high purposes which are the *raison d'être* of the convention.[179]

Indeed it is this specific nature of the convention which has led the ICJ to recognize that the principles underlying the Convention are principles that are recognized by civilized nations as binding on States, even without any conventional obligation,[180] as it states that the Genocide Convention was intended by the General Assembly and by the contracting parties to be universal in scope as it was approved by a resolution that was unanimously adopted by fifty-six States.[181]

Thus in the Vidoge Blagojevic and Dragan Jokic case, the Trial Chamber citing the Appeals Chamber's judgment in the Jelisic case says that the specific intent requires that the perpetrator seeks to achieve the destruction, in whole or in part, of a national, ethnical, racial or religious group, as such.[182] The Akayesu case explains the concept of special intent saying it is the key element of an intentional offense, which offense is characterized by a

177 Idem, para 187

178 Report of the International Law Commission on the work of its forty-eighth session, p 44

179 ICJ advisory opinion, 1951, p 12

180 Reservations to the Convention on the Prevention and Punishment of the Crime of Genocide, Advisory Opinion, I.C.J. Reports 1951, p. 12

181 Idem

182 ICTY, Prosecutor v. Vidoge Blago Blagojevic, Dragan Jokic, Trial Chamber, 17.01.2005, para 656

psychological relationship between the physical result and the mental state of the perpetrator.[183]

The Tribunal clarifies that the act must have been committed against one or several individuals, because such individual or individuals were members of a specific group, and specifically because they belonged to this group, indeed referring to the submission of the representative of Brazil during the travaux préparatoires the Tribunal said that:

> [G]enocide is characterized by the factor of particular intent to destroy a group. In the absence of that factor, whatever the degree of atrocity of an act and however similar it might be to the acts described in the convention, that act could still not be called genocide.[184]

3.4 In Whole or in Part

In the Kamuhanda case the Trial Chamber found that in order to establish intent to destroy "in whole or in part", it is not necessary to show that the perpetrator intended to achieve the complete annihilation of a group from every corner of the globe. It is sufficient to prove that the perpetrator has intended to destroy more than an imperceptible number of the targeted group.[185]

However, the Vidoge Blagojevic and Dragan Jokic case specifies that the numeric size of the targeted part of the group should be evaluated with the overall size of the entire group, as well as the prominence within the group of the targeted portion.[186] It goes without that there should be a proportionality between the targeted group and the victims which means the numerical size of the protected and the numerical size of the attacked members of the group.

Neither the convention nor the jurisprudence has attempted to give figures to be considered. Indeed such a venture would rather be counterproductive, as each case is to be dealt with on a case-by-case basis.

---

183 ICTR, Akayesu v. Prosecutor, Trial ChamberJudgement para 518

184 Idem, para 519

185 Idem, para 628

186 Idem, para 668

3.5 The Barayagwiza Trial

According to a witness name-coded AHB, a Hutu farmer, who testified that:

> [H]e saw Barayagwiza in 1994 in Gisenyi, one week after the plane crash. Barayagwiza arrived at around noon in a red vehicle, together with another vehicle, a white Daihatsu, and parked in front of Ntamaherezo's house. Ntamaherezo, who was the MRND President in the commune, distributed weapons in 1994. That morning Ntamaherezo had told them that Barayagwiza would be arriving with tools to kill the Tutsi. When he arrived, Barayagwiza got out of the car. *Impuzamugambi* wearing CDR caps got out of the Daihatsu and offloaded firearms and machetes into Ntamaherezo's house. Witness AHB knew these *Impuzamugambi* and named them Sinanrugu and Nzabandora, both cellule officials. During this time Barayagwiza was talking to Ntamaherezo, and Witness AHB was twenty steps away from them. Barayagwiza and some of the *Impuzamugambi* left after ten minutes. Other *Impuzamugambi* and others who were waiting took the weapons away and used them to kill. On that same day, Witness AHB saw Sinanrugu and Nzabandora kill thirty people, including children and older people.[187]

Based on the above given testimony the Trial Chamber made a finding that Barayagwiza was involved in planning the killing but also that he supervised roadblocks manned by the *Impuzamugambi*, established to stop and kill Tutsi.[188]

As for genocidal intent, the Trial Chamber drew his genocidal intent from statements he had made in a public rally. Jean-Bosco Barayagwiza said in public meetings: "Let's exterminate them" with "them" being understood by those who heard it as a reference to the Tutsi population. After separating the Tutsi from the Hutu and humiliating the Tutsi by forcing them to perform the *Ikinyemera*, their traditional dance, at several public meetings, Barayagwiza threatened to kill them and said it would not be difficult.[189]

---

[187] See ICTR, Prosecutor v. Nahimana et al., Trial Chamber Judgment, para 720

[188] Idem, para 954

[189] Idem, para 967

Thus the Tribunal concluded that from his words and deeds, Barayagwiza's ruthless commitment to the destruction of the Tutsi population as a means by which to protect the political gains secured by the Hutu majority from 1959 is evident.[190] This conclusion however might seem to be misplaced. It is one thing to aim at making political gains it is another to aim to commit acts of genocide. Furthermore, as much as separating Tutsi from Hutu and forcing them to perform their cultural dance is highly degrading and humiliating it does not have on its own a genocidal intent. The Tribunal's reasoning should have been articulated from the statement of the accused particularly the call for extermination made public as it will be discussed later.

3.6 The Barayagwiza Appeal

Taking the matter before the Appeals Chamber, the Defense contended that the finding of the Trial Chamber was erroneous. First, the Defense submitted that the following facts have not been established: (1) the use of the expression "*tubatsembatsembe*" or "let's exterminate them"; and (2) his acts and utterances against the Bagogwe Tutsi.[191]

The Appeals Chamber referred to the existing jurisprudence and stated that:

> The jurisprudence accepts that in most cases genocidal intent will be proved by circumstantial evidence. In such cases, it is necessary that the finding that the accused had genocidal intent be the only reasonable inference from the totality of the evidence.[192]

Indeed, whereas the Trial Chamber had found that Barayagwiza had genocidal intent based on the fact that he said "let's exterminate them" at public meetings, "them" being understood by those who heard it as a reference to the Tutsi population; his threats and intimidations towards the Bagogwe Tutsi; and more generally, his involvement in RTLM and the CDR, which both conveyed an explicitly genocidal discourse.[193]

---

190 Idem, para 967

191 ICTR, Prosecutor v. Nahimana et al., Appeals Chamber Judgment, para 528

192 Idem, para 524

193 Idem, para 727

The Appeals Chamber found that the Trial Chamber could reasonably conclude from the totality of the evidence relied on by it that, at CDR meetings, Appellant Barayagwiza had himself used slogans calling for the extermination of Tutsi, such as "*gutsembatsemba*", "*tuzabatsembatsemba*" and "*tuzitsembatsembe*" and that the use of these expressions was a determining fact to prove his genocidal intent.[194]

[194] Idem, para 939

CHAPTER 4

INCHOATE CRIMES

Article 3 of the 1948 Convention against Genocide provides that:

> The following acts shall be punishable:
> (a) Genocide;
> (b) Conspiracy to commit genocide;
> (c) Direct and public incitement to commit genocide;
> (d) Attempt to commit genocide;
> (e) Complicity in genocide.[195]

In general terms, criminal law establishes a difference between a substantive crime and a mode of liability. Thus, it is settled that an act of complicity falls short of being a criminal activity in itself however such acts are still punishable as without the assistance of the accomplice the crime might not have been committed the way it was committed as it might not have been committed altogether. In this case, an accomplice is punished as an accessory to the principal who is the main offender.[196]

The purpose of the above-cited article 3 seems unclear considering that it has listed the substantive crime of genocide and a mode of liability, namely complicity in genocide under the same category. It is however clear that the law intended to criminalize two inchoate crimes, conspiracy to commit genocide and direct and public incitement to commit genocide.

A quick reading of Article 3 which provides for punishable acts under the convention would suggest that such acts are considered substantive crimes on their own as the article provides for the legal basis for their prosecution. Such reading might sound correct as far as conspiracy and direct and public incitement are concerned. Under no circumstance would complicity in

---

195 The same has been captured under Article 2(3) of the ICTR Statute.

196 For more details on criminal participation see Gracieux Mbuzukongira, Aiding and Abetting by Omission: Special Focus on Mode of Participation to the Crime of Extermination in the Rutaganira Case, Galda-Verlage, 2019

genocide be prosecuted as a substantive crime irrespective of the fact that article three would seem to provide for the same.

A meaningful interpretation of the article would understand the wish of the legislator as having been to ensure that any act of complicity is rather punished nevertheless as participation and not as a substantive crime. In other words, the provision of Article 3(e) does not have any implication on how complicity should be prosecuted. Indeed even Article 3(a) would appear redundant as Article 2 has already offered a legal basis for the prosecution of the crime of genocide.

Furthermore, as the rules of criminal law have already established that any attempt to commit any crime is punishable as such, article (d) does not add much to the existing legal ground for the prosecution of attempted crimes as by no means can it be considered to change the prescribed rules on attempted crimes.

This chapter will therefore be focused on a legal discussion of the remaining provisions of article 3 namely article 3(b) providing for conspiracy to commit genocide and article 3(c) providing for direct and public incitement to commit genocide.

4.1 Conspiracy to Commit Genocide

Etymologically the word conspiracy derives its origin from two Latin words, ''*corf* and "*spirare*" meaning to breathe together.[197] Thus conspiracy to commit genocide is understood as an agreement between two or more persons to commit the crime of genocide.[198]

The travaux preparatoires of the 1948 Convention explains why they prohibit conspiracy to commit genocide under any form and public, direct incitement to genocide, whether followed or not by genocide. Accordingly, it is stated that considering that the crime of genocide is of extreme gravity and how its effects cause irreparable damages, considering further that the commission of this crime requires contribution from numerous people,[199] any

---

197 Per Leonard Hand, J, *Harrison* v. U.S. 1 F.2d 259, 263 (2d Cir. 1925). As cited by Mohamed C. Othman, accountability for international humanitarian law violations, The case of Rwanda and east Timor, Springer 2005, p 192

198 Song Tianying, Conspiracy to Commit Genocide and its Exclusion From the ICC Statute, FICHL Policy Brief Series No. 18, 2014, p 1

199 Indeed the Travaux preparatoires indicate that: Il est necessaire de frapper le seul fait de l'association et de l'entente en vue de l'accomplissement d'actes de genocide. See UNGA, Commission charge d'etudier le developpement progressif de droit international et sa codification, A/AC.10/42 du 06.06.1947

act that lead to the commission of genocide would be better punished whether indeed genocide has occurred or not.

It is important to note that the Convention on the Prevention and Punishment of the Crime of Genocide has assigned itself a double mandate that is to punish the crime of genocide whenever it occurs but also to prevent its commission whenever possible. Amongst other strategies, the preventive mission can be accomplished by criminalizing certain behavior even before the crime itself is committed. This would explain the nature of inchoate crimes which are considered independent crimes as they remain crimes even before the crime is committed and are punishable as such.

A discussion on the closely related rules governing attempts to commit genocide will fall out of the scope of this research suffice noting that a case of attempted genocide requires the commencement of the execution of criminal activities. The same goes for a joint criminal enterprise which requires that in addition to the agreement, the parties to the agreement should have taken certain actions in the performance of the agreement, however, the next section will rather be focused on the constitutive elements of the crime of conspiracy to commit genocide.

4.1.1 Constitutive Elements

As it was said in the Nyiramasuhuko et al., case, the Appeals Chamber indicated that:

> [W]hen an accused is charged with conspiracy to commit genocide according to Article 2(3)(b) of the Statute, the Prosecution must plead in the indictment:
>
> (i) an agreement between individuals aimed at the commission of genocide; and
> (ii) the fact that the individuals taking part in the agreement possessed the intent to destroy in whole or in part, a national, ethnic, racial, or religious group, as such.[200]

However the crucial question of proof of such agreement was addressed in Popovic case and the Appeals Chamber found that while the *actus reus* of conspiracy to commit genocide can be proved by evidence of meetings to plan genocide, it can also be inferred from other evidence. In particular, a concerted

200 ICTR, Prosecutor v. Nyiramasuhuko et al., Appeals Chamber Judgment, para 469

agreement to commit genocide may be inferred from the conduct of the conspirators which on its own constitutes circumstantial evidence for instance the highly coordinated manner in which the crimes were committed.[201]

Thus, as indicated in the Gatete case in which the Appeals Chamber held that:

> [T]he crime of genocide has a materially distinct *actus reus* from the crime of conspiracy to commit genocide and both crimes are based on different underlying conduct. The crime of genocide requires the commission of one of the enumerated acts in Article 2(2) of the Statute, while the crime of conspiracy to commit genocide requires the act of agreeing to commit genocide.[202]

As for the mens rea for the crime of conspiracy to commit, the persons involved in the agreement must possess the mens rea for genocide, that is the intent to destroy in whole or in part a national, ethnic, racial, or religious group as such.[203]

4.1.2 Cumulative Sentencing

One of the most unsettled questions within the jurisprudence is the question of whether and/or under which conditions can cumulative sentencing be entered for the crime of conspiracy to commit genocide and the crime of genocide itself.

Understood from the perspective of inchoate crimes, that is, incomplete crimes, as earlier discussed, they aim at the preventive role and are designed to be punished even if the main crime did not occur. However, when the statute provides for such crime as an independent crime, from a plain reading of the law, nothing would prevent the Tribunal from entering a cumulative sentence for two crimes that are provided for by two separate legal provisions.

The lack of clarity on these two legal views within the Convention and the subsequent statutes of the ad-hoc tribunals which adopted mutatis mutandis in the text of the Convention has led to a lack of uniformity within the jurisprudence on this particular question.

---

201 ICTY, Prosecutor Popovic et al., Appeals Chamber Judgment, para 533, See ICTR, Prosecutor v. Callixte Nzabonimana, Trial Chamber Judgment, para 1739

202 ICTR, Prosecutor v. Gatete, Appeals Chamber Judgment, para 260

203 ICTR, Prosecutor v. Gatete, Trial Chamber Judgment, para 611

Indeed, in the Nzabonimana case, the Trial Chamber took note of the split of authority regarding whether convictions may be entered simultaneously for conspiracy to commit genocide and for genocide, referring Gatete, and Popović et al., cases. Nevertheless, the Chamber stressed that it did not need to address this issue because the conduct that serves as the basis for conspiracy to commit genocide is different from the conduct that serves as the basis for genocide as hereunder discussed.[204]

The other not less pertinent aspect of the crime of genocide is that from its very nature, the crime of genocide cannot be committed by random criminals acting independently. This crime requires a minimum level of coordination and prior mutual understanding among the criminals. This would imply that at any point that the crime of genocide will have happened there will always be a prior agreement amongst the criminals although virtually the reverse of this assumption will not be always true.

The consequence of the above reasoning would mean that every accused of the crime of genocide could be potentially accused of conspiracy to commit genocide. Thus in the Gatete case, the Trial Chamber found that the accused entered into an agreement to commit genocide. However, it reasoned that given that a conviction for genocide, and not also conspiracy to commit genocide, in no way lessens the Accused's criminal culpability, the Chamber decided to follow the approach taken by the Popović and Musema Trial Chambers and decided not to enter a conviction for both genocide and conspiracy to commit genocide.[205]

Nevertheless, the Trial Chamber's decision was reversed by the Appeals Chamber, which refers to the findings of the Trial Chamber's decision according to which the facts underpinning the elements of conspiracy to commit genocide have been proven, did not find it redundant to enter a conviction for conspiracy to commit genocide as it did.[206]

In the Musema case, the Trial Chamber held that the accused

> does not incur criminal responsibility for the crime of conspiracy to commit genocide, under Count 3, all the more so as, based on the same acts, the Prosecutor presented evidence of Musema's participation in the commission of genocide, the substantive offense concerning the conspiracy.[207]

---

204 See ICTR, Prosecutor v. Callixte Nzabonimana, Trial Chamber Judgment, footnote 2184

205 ICTR, Prosecutor v. Gatete, Trial Chamber Judgment, paras 661-662

206 ICTR, Prosecutor v. Gatete, Appeals Chamber Judgment, para 265

207 ICTR, Prosecutor v. Alfred Musema, Trial Chamber Judgment, para 941

It is in that vein, in same the Musema case that the Appeals Chamber citing the Celebici case concluded that multiple criminal convictions entered under different statutory provisions are permissible only if each statutory provision involved has a materially distinct element not contained in the other.[208] The Chamber further indicated that an element is materially distinct from another if it requires proof of a fact not required by the other.[209]

Thus, in the Nyiramasuhuko case, the Trial Chamber entered convictions for conspiracy to commit genocide and genocide. Nyiramasuhuko was found guilty of conspiracy to commit genocide, for entering into an agreement with other members of the Interim Government on or after 9 April 1994 to kill Tutsis in Butare prefecture, as she was found guilty of genocide for ordering the killing of Tutsis taking refuge at the Butare prefecture office.[210]

4.1.3 The Baragwiza Trial

The Trial Chamber found that there were several triangular links as well among the three institutions effectively controlled by the three co-accused, namely the Newspaper *Kangura* interacted extensively with both the local radio station RTLM and a particular political party CDR. The Trial Chamber referred to an article signed by Ngeze and published in *Kangura* in January 1994 linking three institutions which accordingly stated that: "*Kangura* has been supported by CDR and then RTLM radio station was established… The entire Hutu youth now have been taught how the Hutu youth can confront the *Inyenzis*…".[211]

The Trial Chamber found further that it was established beyond a reasonable doubt, that Nahimana, Barayagwiza, and Ngeze consciously interacted with each other, using the institutions they controlled to promote a joint agenda, which was the targeting of the Tutsi population for destruction.[212]

In the Baragwiza case, the Trial Chamber drew his mens rea for the crime of conspiracy to commit genocide from the fact that:

> Jean-Bosco Barayagwiza said in public meetings: "Let's exterminate them" with "them" being understood by those

208 ICTR, Prosecutor v. Alfred Musema, Appeals Chamber Judgment, para 361
209 Idem
210 ICTR, Prosecutor v. Nyaramasuhuko, Summary of Judgment and Sentence, 24.06. 2011, para 38-39
211 ICTR, Prosecutor v. Nahimana et al., Trial Chamber Judgment, para 1053
212 Idem, para 1054

> who heard it as a reference to the Tutsi population. After separating the Tutsi from the Hutu and humiliating the Tutsi by forcing them to perform the *Ikinyemera*, their traditional dance, at several public meetings, Barayagwiza threatened to kill them and said it would not be difficult.[213]

Thus the Trial Chamber found that Nahimana, Ngeze, and Barayagwiza, all three co-accused in the media case through personal collaboration as well as interaction among institutions within their control, namely RTLM, *Kangura*, and CDR, guilty of conspiracy to commit genocide under Article 2(3)(b) and according to Article 6(1) of the Statute.[214]

4.1.4 The Barayagwiza Appeal

Before the Appeals Chambe, the Appellants contended that the evidence of their personal collaboration does not establish an agreement to commit genocide. Indeed, Appellants Nahimana and Ngeze submitted that the Trial Chamber's findings in regard to the content of the meetings between the Appellants are not supported by any evidence.[215] They denied that there was any "interaction among institutions", and submitted that, even if there had been, that would not establish beyond reasonable doubt that those who controlled those institutions had come to an agreement to commit genocide.[216]

It is established that in the absence of any evidence of an agreement to commit genocide, the tribunal can consider circumstantial evidence for the same. However such evidence should be of a high threshold. Thus in the Baragwiza the Appeals Chamber found that:

> There is no doubt, in the Appeals Chamber's view, that the aforementioned factual findings are compatible with the existence of "a joint agenda" aiming at committing genocide. However, it is not the only reasonable inference. A reasonable trier of fact could also find that these institutions had interacted to promote the ideology of "Hutu power" in the context of a political struggle between Hutu and Tutsi, or

---

213 Idem, para 967

214 Idem, para 1055

215 ICTR, Prosecutor v. Nahimana et al., Appeals Chamber Judgment, para 902

216 Idem, para 903

> to disseminate ethnic hatred against the Tutsi without going as far as the destruction in whole or in part, of that group.[217]

Subsequently, The Appeal Chamber did set aside the conviction on conspiracy to commit genocide.[218] Indeed when based on circumstantial evidence, the finding of a conspiracy must be the only reasonable inference that can be made based on the totality of the evidence.

4.2 Direct and Public Incitement

The crime of direct and public incitement is constituted by a material element of incitement, which the civil law system refers to as public provocation is indeed the fact of directly and publicly inciting the commission of genocide whereas the psychological element is the genocidal intent that is the inciter intent to cause others to commit genocide. The Akayesu case says that it implies a desire on the part of the perpetrator to create by his actions a particular state of mind necessary to commit genocide in the minds of the people they are inciting.[219]

From the wording of the law, the *actus reus* requires two aspects, which are direct and public. The Akayesu case citing the International Law Commission works indicates that the element of direct incitement requires specifically urging another individual to take immediate criminal action rather than merely making a vague or indirect suggestion.[220] Whereas, the element of public incitement would require a call for criminal action to several individuals, in a public place, or to members of the general public at large. Thus, an individual may communicate the call for criminal action in person in a public place or by technical means of mass communication, such as by radio or television.[221]

The Barayagwiza case having been joined with Ferdinand Nahimana and Hassan Ngeze, to be famously referred to as the media case addresses

---

217 Idem, para 910

218 Idem, para 912

219 ICTR, Prosecutor v. Akayesu Trial Chamber Judgment.

220 Draft Code of Crimes Against the Peace and Security of Mankind, art. 2(3)(f); Report of the International Law Commission to the General Assembly, 51 U.N. ORGA Supp. (No. 10), at 26, U.N. Doc. A/51/10(1996) as cited in ICTR, Prosecutor v. Akayesu Trial Chamber Judgment, footnote 128

221 Draft Code of Crimes Against the Peace and Security of Mankind, art. 2(3)(f); Report of the International Law Commission to the General Assembly, 51 U.N. ORGA Supp. (No. 10), at 26, U.N. Doc. A/51/10(1996). Akayesu TC footnote 126

the crime of incitement at length. Thus the Trial Chamber started by citing the Julius Steicher case, as hereunder discussed. Much that the Statute of the IMT of Nuremberg does not provide directly for the crime of incitement, its Article 6 provides valid legal to punish leaders, organizers, instigators, etc... some individuals were successfully prosecuted amongst other things for what they and/ or published for instance Julius Streicher was accused to speaking publicly in support of the Jewish pogrom which was taking place at that time. Indeed the judgment reads that:

> For his twenty-five years of speaking, writing, and preaching hatred of the Jews, Streicher was widely known as "Jew-Baiter Number One." In his speeches and articles, week after week, month after month, he infected the German mind with the virus of anti-Semitism, and incited the German people to active persecution.[222]

Amongst other crimes he was accused of were the following acts:

> In an article published by *Der Sturmer* in May 1939, he wrote: A punitive expedition must come against the Jews in Russia. A punitive expedition that will provide the same fate for them that every murderer and criminal must expect. Death sentence and execution. The Jews in Russia must be killed. They must be exterminated root and branch.[223]

Furthermore, the records of *Der Sturmer* indicate a total of twenty-six articles, published between August 1941 and September 1944, twelve by Streicher's hand, which demanded annihilation and extermination in unequivocal terms. He wrote and published on 25th December 1941: "If the danger of the reproduction of that curse of God in the Jewish blood is to finally come to an end, then there is only one way-the extermination of those people whose father is the devil."[224] And in February 1944, his article stated: " Whoever does what a Jew does is a scoundrel, a criminal. And he who repeats and wishes to copy him deserves the same fate, annihilation, death."[225]

---

[222] Streicher Judgement, Lillian Goldman Law Library, 2008, available on https://avalon.law.yale.edu/imt/judstrei.asp, last consulted on 06.12.2023

[223] Idem

[224] Idem

[225] Idem

The tribunal took note of the fact that each issue of *Der Sturmer*, would reach a wide audience of 600,000 readers in 1935, the Tribunal found that Streicher's incitement to murder and extermination at the time when Jews in the East were being killed under the most horrible conditions constitutes persecution on political and racial grounds in connection with war crimes as defined by the Charter, and constitutes a crime against humanity.

This judgment however suffers many weaknesses. Whereas the Nuremberg Charter provides for instigation as a mode of liability, Mr Streicher was sentenced for incitement to murder and extermination which is not provided for within the Charter as a crime. The difference between the two concepts is not just a matter of mere semantics. Indeed instigation as a mode of liability would require that the crime for which the instigator has instigated is committed, which was the case with Mr. Streicher. This is not the case when it comes to incitement which is an independent crime and is considered committed even when the act incited for is not committed, as it is an inchoate crime for which there must be a legal basis before a sentence is entered.

For instance, article 6(1) of the Statute of the ICTR which provides for the criminal responsibility provides that a person who planned, instigated etc [...] shall be individually responsible for the crime. Whereas article 2(3) (c) lists direct and public incitement to commit genocide among the punishable acts.

Perhaps another challenging element would be the audience to whom the two concepts are directed at. Whereas instigating, like soliciting is usually addressed to a well-known audience either a person or a particular group of people. Incitement is addressed to a public which might even be unknown to the person inciting them for instance through radio or newspapers publication.

This need to be distinguished from the closely related but different crime of hate speech which is currently not provided for under the international law framework but is generally understood as being constituted by the fact of depicting negatively a group of people, without calling for further action against them.[226]

In the Streicher case, for the Tribunal to enter a sentence based on instigation it needed to establish a link between the accused and the people

---

226 Wibke Kristin Timmermann, Incitement in international criminal law, International Review of the Red Cross, Volume 88 Number 864 December 2006, p 847

who perpetrated various acts he was accused of, which the Tribunal was not able to do, and for it to enter as indicated earlier a sentence on the ground of incitement it needed a legal basis for the same and it didn't have any.

The Trial Chamber further refer to the Hans Fritzsche case who was rather acquitted by Tribunal as he opposed any policy that would incite Germans to commit criminal conduct and he never propagated the master race theory.

4.2.1 The Barayagwiza Trial

The Trial Chamber found that Jean-Bosco Barayagwiza was one of the principal founders of CDR and played a leading role in its formation and development, which promoted the killing of Tutsi civilians. The Trial Chamber found that this was evidenced by the chanting of "tubatsembatsembe" or "let's exterminate them", by Barayagwiza himself and by CDR members and *Impuzamugambi* in his presence at public meetings and demonstrations.[227]

The Trial Chamber would further find that the direct involvement of Barayagwiza in the call for genocide from the fact that Barayagwiza was at the organizational helm of CDR and from the fact that He was also on-site at the meetings, demonstrations, and roadblocks that created an infrastructure for the killing of Tutsi civilians. This reasoning is however problematic in the sense that his presence at the roadblock cannot be connected to the crime of direct and public incitement to commit genocide as these two conducts are not connected.

Thus the Trial Chamber found Barayagwiza guilty of direct and public incitement to genocide under Article 2(3)(c) of its Statute, under Article 6(1) of its Statute. The Chamber found that Barayagwiza had superior responsibility over members of CDR and the *Impuzamugambi*.[228] For his failure to take necessary and reasonable measures to prevent the acts of direct and public incitement to commit genocide caused by CDR members, the Chamber found Barayagwiza guilty of direct and public incitement to commit genocide pursuant to Article 6(3) of its Statute.[229]

---

227 ICTR, Prosecutor v. Nahimana et al., Trial Chamber Judgment 1035

228 Idem

229 Idem

4.2.2 The Barayagwiza Appeal

In his appeal, Barayagwiza submitted that, in order to prove that he had superior responsibility under Article 6(3), it was necessary for the Prosecutor to prove the following:

1. that he had a *dolus specialis*;
2. that he had superior responsibility for CDR members; and
3. that CDR members killed Tutsi civilians.[230]

Thus the Defense pleaded that even in the event that is considered that the Appellant was National President of the CDR, this would not imply that he was the hierarchical superior of the CDR militants, in the absence of a showing by the Trial Chamber that his powers met the criterion of effective control to trigger his criminal responsibility under Article 6(3).[231]

Accordingly, the Appeals Chamber did set aside the Appellant's conviction under Article 6(3) of the Statute for direct and public incitement to commit genocide on account of acts by CDR militants and *Impuzamugambi*[232] and reversed convictions of Appellant Barayagwiza based on Article 6(1) of the Statute for the crimes of direct and public incitement to commit genocide for his acts within the CDR and conspiracy to commit genocide, as well as his convictions based on Article 6(3) of the Statute in respect of his acts within RTLM and the CDR for the crimes of genocide, direct and public incitement to commit genocide.[233]

Concluding Remarks

As far as the principle of review in international law is concerned the International Court of Justice has set a standard that meets international expectations. Such a standard should not be deviated from particularly when the laws guiding the said principle are similar. Other international courts and tribunals are therefore called to uphold the same standard.

Unfortunately, whereas the relevant ICTR laws are spelled out, in the Barayagwiza case, the Appeals Chamber decided contrary to its own rules and

230 ICTR, Prosecutor v. Nahimana et al., Appeals Chamber Judgment, para 864
231 Idem, para 879
232 Idem, para 883
233 Idem, p 346

on untanable the grounds. Such a bad precedent is deplorable, considering that the same set of rules emanates from the same judges who had sworn to discharge their duty according to the law.

This situation is worsened by the subsequent cases which seem to consider the poorly reasoned judgment as a relevant authority on the matter. The purpose of this research has been to appeal to judges and other actors to put aside the Barayagwiza judgment and not to consider it as a relevant authority as far as the concept of review is concerned.

Such a decision was a result of the pressure exerted on the ICTR from certain governments whose stand on the outcome of certain cases has never been confidential. However international judges are expected to be individuals of high morality with the ability to administer justice without fear or favor else they should relieve themselves from such duties.

This is crucial not just a matter of personal dignity but the future of the entire international criminal justice would depend on its current outcome, the less justice is seen to be done currently the less public trust will attract the entire international criminal justice in the future. It is on record that most African parliaments have considered in one way or another a motion to withdraw from the Rome Statute following the highly applauded move of Burundi, the international community needs to understand factors that underline such a move.

Indeed such a move is mainly dictated by the perception that international criminal justice is politicized and that cases are decided based on weaponized justice which is dictated by political, financial, or other strategic interests but not by legal considerations.

Unless this situation is rectified the future of the entire international criminal justice is at stake. The ultimate purpose of this research is rather an individual contribution to the process of rectification of the said system for its survival and not otherwise.

It is hard to understand that an international judge could enter a sentence for a crime as serious as the crime of genocide based on the testimony of one witness if one considers the financial, and human resources allocated to an institution as the ICTR, let alone the time this trial had taken.

Such hasty judgment has coasted a great deal of credibility to the system. However, this is a call to various officers entrusted with the noble call to discharge international justice to honor their call and contribute to the advancement of international law and not otherwise as it has been the case in the Barayagwiza trial.

SELECTED BIBLIOGRAPHY

Published Works

Antonin Scalia and Bryan A. Garner, Reading Law, The Interpretation of Legal Texts, Thomson/West, 2012

Antonio Cassese, International Criminal Law, Oxford University Press, 2003

Emanuala Fronza and Stefano Manacorda, La justice penale international dans les decisions des tribunaux adhoc, Etudes des law clinic en droit penal international, Dalloz, 2003

David Lisson, Defining "national group" in the genocide convention: A case study for Timor-Leste, Stanford Law review, Vol 60, 2008

De Smith, Woolf& Jowell, Judicial Review of Administrative Action, 5th ed

Dzhangir Kerimov, *Methology of Law*, Progress Publishers, 1989

Ernst Freund, Interpretation of Statutes, 65 U. Pa. L. Rev. 207, 218, 1917

Kittichaisaree, International criminal law, Oxford University Press, 2005

Kriangsak Kittichaisaree, International criminal law, Oxford University Press, 2005

Machteld Boot, Genocide, Crimes against humanity and war crimes, 2002

Patrick Riley, A treatise of legal philosophy and general jurisprudence, the philosophers" philosophy of law from the seventeenth century to our days, Springer, 2009

Nathaniel Lindley, An introduction to the study of jurisprudence, Hodges and Smith, 1955

Reza Banakar and Max Travers, Law, Sociology and Method, *Theory and Method in Socio-Legal Research*, Hart Publishing, 2005

Song Tianying, Conspiracy to Commit Genocide and its Exclusion From the ICC Statute, FICHL Policy Brief Series No. 18, 2014

Suri Ratnapala, Jurisprudence, Cambridge University Press, 2009

Wibke Kristin Timmermann, Incitement in international criminal law, irrc,

Volume 88 Number 864 December 2006

William Schabas, Groups protected by the genocide convention: Conflicting interpretations from the international criminal tribunal for Rwanda, Journal of International & Comparative Law, Vol. 6

Legal and Quasi Legal Sources

1950 UNESCO declaration on the race question

Draft Code of Crimes against the Peace and Security of Mankind

ICC Elements of Crimes

ICC Rules of Procedure and Evidence

ICJ Rules of Court

ICJ Statute of the Court

ICTR Code of Professional Conduct for Defense Counsel

ICTR Directive for the Registry of the ICTR

ICTR Directive on the Assignment of Defense Counsel

ICTR Prosecutor's Regulations and Code of Conduct (1999)

ICTR Rules of Procedure and Evidence

ICTR Statute of the International Criminal Tribunal for Rwanda

Report of the International Commission of Inquiry on Darfur to the United Nations Secretary-General, UN Doc. S/2005/60, 25 January 2005

Report of the International Law Commission on the work of its forty-eighth session

Report of the International Law Commission to the General Assembly, 51 U.N. ORGA Supp. (No. 10), at 26, U.N. Doc. A/51/10(1996)

Rome Statute of the International Criminal Court

The Charter of the International Military Tribunal of Nuremberg

List of Cases

Cour International de Justice, Affaire de la demande en revision de l'arret du 11 Septembre 1992 en l'affaire du differend frontalier terrestre, insulaire et maritime, El Salvador c. Hondras

ICJ, Application for revision and interpretation of the Judgment of 24 February 1982 in the case concerning the Continental Shelf, Tunisia v. Libyan Arab Jamahiriya

ICJ, Application for revision of the Judgment of 23 May 2008 in the case concerning sovereignty over Pedra/Pulau Batu Piteh, Middle Rocks and South Ledge, Malaysia/Singapore

ICJ, Croatia v. Serbia

ICJ, Reservations to the Convention on the Prevention and Punishment of the Crime of Genocide, Advisory Opinion, 1951

ICTR Appeals Chamber Decision on review and/or reconsideration, 14.09.2000

ICTR Prosecutor v. Clement Kayishema and Obed Ruzindana

ICTR Prosecutor v. Jean Bosco Barayagwiza, Decision on the Prosecutor's request for review or reconsideration, 31.03.2000

ICTR, Prosecutor v. Afred Musema

ICTR, Prosecutor v. Akayesu

ICTR, Prosecutor v. Bagilishema

ICTR, Prosecutor v. Callixte Nzabonimana

ICTR, Prosecutor v. Gatete

ICTR, Prosecutor v. Georges Anderson Nderubumwe Rutaganda

ICTR, Prosecutor v. Karemera

ICTR, Prosecutor v. Nyiramasuhuko et al.,

ICTR, Prosecutor v. Rutaganda

ICTR, Prosecutor v. Semanza

ICTR, Prosecutor v. Seromba

ICTY, Prosecutor v. JadrankoPRLIC et al.

ICTY, Prosecutor v Krstic

ICTY, Prosecutor v Slobodan Milosevic

ICTY, Prosecutor v. Blagoje Simic et al.

ICTY, Prosecutor v. Dusko Tadic

ICTY, Prosecutor v. Goran Jelisic

ICTY, Prosecutor v. Popovic et al.,

ICTY, Prosecutor v. Radovan Kazadzic

ICTY, Prosecutor v. Tolimir Zdravka

ICTY, Prosecutor v. Veselin Sljiv

ICTY, Prosecutor v. Vidoge Blago Blagojevic and Dragan Jokic

International Court of Justice, Application for revision of the Judgment of 23 May 2008 in the case concerning sovereignty over Pedra/Pulau Batu Piteh, Middle Rocks and South Ledge (Malaysia/Singapore), Order of 29 May 2018

International Court of Justice, Application for Revision of the Judgment of 11 September 1992 in the Case concerning the Land, Island and Maritime Frontier Dispute (El Salvador/Honduras: Nicaragua intervening) (El Salvador v. Honduras)

International Court of Justice, Case concerning application of the convention on the prevention punishment of the crime of genocide, (Bosnia and Jerzegovina v. Serbia and Montenegro)

Kungys v. United States, 485 U.S. 759, 778 (1988)

Military Tribunal I, Transcript of Judgment and Sentence 1948, 10 Mar 48-M-TE-3-1-Gaylord (Int. Treidell) Court I case 8

DISCLAIMER

The 31. 03. 2000 Appeal's decision on the prosecutor's request for review or reconsideration in the Jean Bosco Barayagwiza v. The Prosecutor which is the appendix to this book has been reprinted in accordance with the Access Policy for the Records held by the International Residual Mechanism for Criminal Tribunals (MICT/17/Rev.1)

ICTR-97-19-AR72
7-4-2000
(1481-1406)

1481

Tribunal Pénal International pour le Rwanda
International Criminal Tribunal for Rwanda

UNITED NATIONS
NATIONS UNIES

IN THE APPEALS CHAMBER

Before:	Judge Claude JORDA, Presiding Judge Lal Chand VOHRAH Judge Mohamed SHAHABUDDEEN Judge Rafael NIETO-NAVIA Judge Fausto POCAR
Registrar:	Mr Agwu U OKALI
Order of:	31 March 2000

Jean Bosco BARAYAGWIZA
v
THE PROSECUTOR

Case No: ICTR-97-19-AR72

DECISION

(PROSECUTOR'S REQUEST FOR REVIEW OR RECONSIDERATION)

Counsel for Jean Bosco Barayagwiza

Ms Carmelle Marchessault
Mr David Danielson

Counsel for the Prosecutor

Ms Carla Del Ponte
Mr Bernard Muna
Mr Mohamed Othman
Mr Upawansa Yapa
Mr Sankara Menon
Mr Norman Farrell
Mr Mathias Marcussen

I. INTRODUCTION

1. The Appeals Chamber of the International Criminal Tribunal for the Prosecution of Persons Responsible for Genocide and Other Serious Violations of International Humanitarian Law Committed in the Territory of Rwanda and Rwandan Citizens responsible for genocide and other such violations committed in the territory of neighbouring States, between 1 January and 31 December 1994 ("the Appeals Chamber" and "the Tribunal" respectively) is seised of the "Prosecutor's Motion for Review or Reconsideration of the Appeals Chamber's Decision Rendered on 3 November 1999, in Jean-Bosco Barayagwiza v. the Prosecutor and Request for Stay of Execution" filed by the Prosecutor on 1 December 1999 ("the Motion for Review").

2. The decision sought to be reviewed was issued by the Appeals Chamber on 3 November 1999 ("the Decision"). In the Decision, the Appeals Chamber allowed the appeal of Jean-Bosco Barayagwiza ("the Appellant") against the decision of Trial Chamber II which had rejected his preliminary motion challenging the legality of his arrest and detention. In allowing the appeal, the Appeals Chamber dismissed the indictment against the Appellant with prejudice to the Prosecutor and directed the Appellant's immediate release. Furthermore, a majority of the Appeals Chamber (Judge Shahabuddeen dissenting) directed the Registrar to make the necessary arrangements for the delivery of the Appellant to the authorities of Cameroon, from whence he had been originally transferred to the Tribunal's Detention Centre.

3. The Decision was stayed by Order of the Appeals Chamber[1] in light of the Motion for Review. The Appellant is therefore still in the custody of the Tribunal.

[1] The Decision was first stayed for 7 days pending the filing of the Prosecutor's Motion by the Order of 25 November 1999. By Order of 8 December 1999 the stay was continued pending further order.

II. PROCEDURAL HISTORY

4. The Appellant himself was the first to file an application for review of the Decision. On 5 November 1999 he requested the Appeals Chamber to review item 4 of the disposition in the Decision, which directed the Registrar to make the necessary arrangements for his delivery to the Cameroonian authorities.[2] The Prosecutor responded to the application, asking to be heard on the same point[3], and in response to this the Appellant withdrew his request.[4]

5. Following this series of pleadings, the Government of Rwanda filed a request for leave to appear as *amicus curiae* before the Chamber in order to be heard on the issue of the Appellant's delivery to the authorities of Cameroon.[5] This request was made pursuant to Rule 74 of the Rules of Procedure and Evidence of the Tribunal ("the Rules").

6. On 19 November 1999 the Prosecutor filed a "Notice of Intention to File Request for Review of Decision of the Appeals Chamber of 3 November 1999" ("the Prosecutor's Notice of Intention")[6], informing the Chamber of her intention to file her own request for review of the Decision pursuant to Article 25 of the Statute of the Tribunal, and in the alternative, a "motion for reconsideration". On 25 November, the Appeals Chamber issued an Order staying execution of the Decision for 7 days pending the filing of the Prosecutor's Motion for Review. The Appeals Chamber also ordered that that the direction in the Decision that the Appellant be immediately released was to be read subject to the direction to the Registrar to arrange his delivery to the authorities of Cameroon. On the same day, the Chamber received the Appellant's objections to the Prosecutor's Notice of Intention.[7]

---

[2] *Notice of Review and Stay of Dispositive Order No.4 of the Decision of the Appeals Chamber dated 3rd November 1999*

[3] *Prosecutor's Response to Appellant's Notice of Review and Stay of Dispositive Order No. 4 of the Appeals Chamber Decision rendered on 3 November 1999, in Jean-Bosco Barayagwiza v. the Prosecutor*, filed on 13 November 1999.

[4] *Withdrawal of the Defence's "Notice of Review and Stay of Dispositive Order No.4 of the Decision of the Appeals Chamber dated 3rd November 1999", dated on 5th November 1999*, filed on 18 November 1999.

[5] *Request by the Government of the Republic of Rwanda for Leave to Appear as Amicus Curiae pursuant to Rule 74*, filed on 19 November 1999.

[6] *Notice of Intention to File Request for Review of Decision of the Appeals Chamber of 3 November 1999 (Rule 120 of the Rules of Procedure and Evidence of the International Criminal Tribunal for Rwanda)*

[7] *Extremely Urgent Appellant's Response to the Prosecutor "Notice of Intention to File Request for Review of Decision of the Appeals Chamber of 3 November 1999"*, filed on 24 November 1999.

7. The Prosecutor's Motion for Review was filed within the 7 day time limit, on 1 December 1999. Annexes to that Motion were filed the following day.[8] On 8 December 1999 the Appeals Chamber issued an Order continuing the stay ordered on 25 November 1999 and setting a schedule for the filing of further submissions by the parties. The Prosecutor was given 7 days to file copies of any statements relating to new facts which she had not yet filed. This deadline was not complied with, but additional statements were filed on 16 February 2000, along with an application for the extension of the time-limit.[9] The Appellant objected to this application.[10]

8. The Order of 8 December 1999 further provided that that the Chamber would hear oral argument on the Prosecutor's Motion for Review, and that the Government of Rwanda might appear at the hearing as *amicus curiae* with respect to the modalities of the release of the Appellant, if that question were reached. The Government of Rwanda filed a memorial on this point on 15 February 2000.[11]

9. On 10 December 1999 the Appellant filed four motions: challenging the jurisdiction of the Appeals Chamber to entertain the review proceedings; opposing the request of the Government of Rwanda to appear as *amicus curiae*; asking for clarification of the Order of 8 December and requesting leave to make oral submissions during the hearing on the

[8] A corrigendum to the motion was filed on 20 December 1999. Corrigenda to the annexes were filed on 13 January and 7 February 2000.

[9] *Prosecutor's Motion for Extension of Time to File New Facts*, corrected on 17 February 2000. The Registrar submitted a *Memorandum to the Appeals Chamber from the Registrar, pursuant to rule 33(B), with regard to the Prosecutor's motion for extension of time limit to file new facts* on 21 February 2000, and the Prosecutor filed a *Supplement to "Prosecutor's motion for extension of time to file new facts" in response to memorandum to the Appeals Chamber from the Registrar pursuant to rule 33(B)* on 22 February 2000.

[10] *Extremely urgent appellant's argument in response to the Prosecutor's 16 February 2000 motion to submit new facts in support of motion for review or reconsideration of 3 November 1999 decision*, filed on 28 February 2000. The *Prosecutor's reply to the "extremely urgent appellant's argument in response to the Prosecutor's 16 February 2000 motion to submit new facts in support of motion for review or reconsideration of 3 November decision* was then filed on 7 March 2000.

[11] *Memorial amicus curiae of the Government of the Republic of Rwanda pursuant to Rule 74 of the Rules of Procedure and Evidence.*

Prosecutor's Motion for Review.[12] The Prosecutor filed her response to these motions on 3 February 2000.[13]

10. On 17 December 1999, the Appeals Chamber issued a Scheduling Order[14] clarifying the time-limits set in its previous Order of 8 December 1999 and on 6 January 2000 the Appellant filed his response to the Prosecutor's Motion for Review.

11. Meanwhile, the Appellant had requested the withdrawal of his assigned counsel, Mr. J.P.L. Nyaberi, by letter of 16 December 1999. The Registrar denied his request on 5 January 2000, and this decision was confirmed by the President of the Tribunal on 19 January 2000.[15] The Appellant then filed a motion before the Appeals Chamber insisting on the withdrawal of assigned counsel, and the assignment of new counsel and co-counsel to represent him with regard to the Prosecutor's Motion for Review.[16] The Appeals Chamber granted his request by Order of 31 January 2000. In view of the change of counsel, the Appellant was given until 17 February 2000 to file a new response to the Prosecutor's Motion for Review, such response to replace the earlier response of 6 January 2000. The Prosecutor was given four further days to reply to any new response submitted. Both these documents were duly filed.[17]

12. The oral hearing on the Prosecutor's Motion for Review took place in Arusha on 22 February 2000.

---

[12] *Extremely Urgent Motion of the Defence Challenging the Jurisdiction of the Appeals Chamber to Entertain the Review Proceedings; Extremely Urgent Motion of the Defence in Opposition to the Request by the Government of the Republic of Rwanda for Leave to Appear as Amicus Curiae Pursuant to Rule 74; Extremely Urgent Motion of the Defence for the Clarification and Interpretation of the Appeals Chamber Order of 8 December 1999; Extremely Urgent Motion of the Defence for the Appellant to Give Oral Testimony During the Hearing of ~~the Review~~ on Facts of his Illegal Detention as Proved in the Decision of 3rd November 1999.*

[13] *The Prosecutor's Consolidated Response to Four Defence Motins Filed on 10 December 1999, Following the Order of the Appeals Chamber dated 8 December 1999.*

[14] Filed on 21 December 1999

[15] *Decision on Review in Terms of Article 19(E) of the Directive on Assignment of Defence Counsel*

[16] Requête en extreme urgence en vue du retrait du conseil J.P. Lumumba Nyaberi de la défense de Jean-Bosco Bnarayagwiza (art.20.4,d du Statut; art.45, 45bis, 73, 107 du Règlement), filed on 26 January 2000.

[17] *Appellants' response to Prosecutor's motion for review or reconsideration of the Appeals Chamber decision rendered on 3 November 1999 in Jean-Bosco Barayagwiza v. the Prosecutor and request for stay of execution,* and *Prosecutor's reply to the appellant's response to the Prosecutor's motion for review or reconsideration of the Appeals Chamber decision rendered on 3 November 2999 in Jean-Bosco Barayagwiza v. the Prosecutor and request for stay of execution,* respectively.

III. APPLICABLE PROVISIONS

A. The Statute

Article 25: Review Proceedings

Where a new fact has been discovered which was not known at the time of the proceedings before the Trial Chambers or the Appeals Chamber and which could have been a decisive factor in reaching the decision, the convicted person or the Prosecutor may submit to the International Tribunal for Rwanda an application for review of the judgement.

B. The Rules

Rule 120: Request for Review

Where a new fact has been discovered which was not known to the moving party at the tine of the proceedings before a Chamber, and could not have been discovered through the exercise of due diligence, the defence or, within one year after the final judgement has been pronounced, the Prosecutor, may make a motion to that Chamber, if it can be reconstituted or, failing that, to the appropriate Chamber of the Tribunal for review of the judgement.

Rule 121: Preliminary Examination

If the Chamber which ruled on the matter decides that the new fact, if it had been proven, could have been a decisive factor in reaching a decision, the Chamber shall review the judgement, and pronounce a further judgement after hearing the parties.

IV. SUBMISSIONS OF THE PARTIES

A. The Prosecution Case

13. The Prosecutor relies on Article 25 of the Statute and Rules 120 and 121 of the Rules as the legal basis for the Motion for Review[18]. The Prosecutor bases the Motion for Review primarily on its claimed discovery of new facts[19]. She states that by virtue of Article 25, there are two basic conditions for an Appeals Chamber to reopen and review its decision, namely the discovery of new facts which were unknown at the time of the original proceedings and which could have been a decisive factor in reaching the original decision[20]. The Prosecutor states that the new facts she relies upon affect the totality of the Decision and open it up for review and reconsideration in its entirety.[21]

14. The Prosecutor opposes the submission by the Defence (paragraph 27 below), that Article 25 can only be invoked following a conviction. The Prosecutor submits that the wording "persons convicted... or from the Prosecutor" provides that both parties can bring a request for review under Article 25, and not that such a right only arises on conviction. The Prosecutor submits that there is no requirement that a motion for review can only be brought after final judgement.[22]

15. The "new facts" which the Prosecutor seeks to introduce and rely on in the Motion for Review fall, according to her, into two categories: new facts which were not known or could not have been known to the Prosecutor at the time of the argument before the Appeals Chamber; and facts which although they "may have possibly been discovered by the Prosecutor" at the time, are, she submits, new, as they could not have been known to be part of the factual dispute or relevant to the issues subsequently determined by the Appeals

[18] *Prosecutor's ~~Motion~~ for Review or Reconsideration of the Appeals Chamber Decision Rendered on 3 November 1999, in Jean-Bosco Barayagwiza v. The Prosecutor and Request for Stay of Execution*, filed on 1 December 1999 at § 1.
[19] *Brief in Support of the Prosecutor's Motion for Review of the Appeals Chamber Decision rendered on 3 November 1999 in Jean-Bosco Barayagwiza v. The Prosecutor Following the Orders of the Appeals Chamber dated 25 November 1999*, at §§ 45 and 46.
[20] *Ibid.*, at § 48.
[21] *Ibid.*, at § 46.
[22] Transcript of Hearing in Arusha on 22 February 2000 ("Transcript") at pages 248 *et seq.* See also, *Prosecutor's Reply to the Appellant's Response to the Prosecutor's Motion for Review or Reconsideration of the Appeals Chamber Decision Rendered on 3 November 1999 in Jean-Bosco Barayagwiza v. The Prosecutor and Request for Stay of Execution* (" Reply"), filed on 21 February 2000, at §§ 5-15

Chamber.[23] The Prosecutor in this submission relies on Rules 121, 107, 115, 117, and 5 of the Rules and Article 14 of the Statute. The Prosecutor submits that the determination of whether something is a new fact, is a mixed question of both fact and law that requires the Appeals Chamber to apply the law as it exists to the facts to determine whether the standard has been met. It does not mean that a fact which occurred prior to the trial cannot be a new fact, or a "fact not discoverable through due diligence."[24]

16. The Prosecutor alleges that numerous factual issues were raised for the first time on appeal by the Appeals Chamber, *proprio motu*, without a full hearing or adjudication of the facts by the Trial Chamber,[25] and contends that the Prosecutor cannot be faulted for failing to comprehend the full nature of the facts required by the Appeals Chamber. Indeed, the Prosecutor alleges that the questions raised did not correspond in full to the subsequent factual determinations by the Appeals Chamber and that at no time was the Prosecutor asked to address the factual basis of the application of the abuse of process doctrine relied upon by the Appeals Chamber in the Decision[26]. The Prosecutor further submits that application of this doctrine involved consideration of the public interest in proceeding to trial and therefore facts relevant to the interests of international justice are new facts on the review.[27] The Prosecutor alleges that she was not provided with the opportunity to present such facts before the Appeals Chamber.[28]

17. In application of the doctrine of abuse of process, the Prosecutor submits that the remedy of dismissal with prejudice was unjustified, as the delay alleged was, contrary to the findings in the Decision, not fully attributable to the Prosecutor.[29] New facts relate to the application of this doctrine and the remedy, which was granted in the Decision.

18. The Prosecutor submits that the Appeals Chamber can also reconsider the Decision, pursuant to its inherent power as a judicial body, to vary or rescind its previous orders, maintaining that such a power is vital to the ability of a court to function properly.[30] She

[23] *Supra* note 19 at § 49.
[24] Transcript at page 253-256.
[25] The Prosecutor alleges that these new facts arose as a result of questions asked by the Appeals Chamber in its Scheduling Order of 3 June 1999. See supra note 19 at §§ 29, 50-54, 147 and158.
[26] *Ibid.*, §§ 54-55.
[27] *Ibid.*, § 56.
[28] *Ibid.*, at § 62.
[29] *Ibid.*, §§ 57-62. In making this submission, the Prosecutor refers to §§ 75, 76, 86, 98-100 and 106 of the Decision.
[30] *Ibid.*, §§ 63- 65.

asserts that this inherent power has been acknowledged by both Tribunals and cites several decisions in support. The Prosecutor maintains that a judicial body can vary or rescind a previous order because of a change in circumstances and also because a reconsideration of the matter has led it to conclude that a different order would be appropriate.[31] In the view of the Prosecutor, although the jurisprudence of the Tribunal indicates that a Chamber will not reconsider its decision if there are no new facts or if the facts adduced could have been relied on previously, where there are facts or arguments of which the Chamber was not aware at the time of the original decision and which the moving party was not in a position to inform the Chamber of at the time of the original decision, a Chamber has the inherent authority to entertain a motion for reconsideration.[32] The Prosecutor asks the Appeals Chamber to exercise its inherent power where an extremely important judicial decision is made without the full benefit of legal argument on the relevant issues and on the basis of incomplete facts.[33]

19. The Prosecutor submits that although a final judgement becomes *res judicata* and subject to the principle of *non bis in idem*, the Decision was not a final judgement on the merits of the case.[34]

20. The Prosecutor submits that she could not have been reasonably expected to anticipate all the facts and arguments which turned out to be relevant and decisive to the Appeals Chamber's Decision.[35]

21. The Prosecutor submits that the new facts offered could have been decisive factors in reaching the Decision, in that had they been available in the record on appeal, they may have altered the findings of the Appeals Chamber that: (a) the period of provisional detention was impermissibly lengthy; (b) there was a violation of Rule 40*bis* through failure to charge promptly; (c) there was a violation of Rule 62 and the right to an initial appearance without delay; and (d) there was failure by the Prosecutor in her obligations to prosecute the case with due diligence. In addition, they could have altered the findings in

[31] *Ibid.*, § 66.
[32] *Ibid.*, §§ 70-73.
[33] *Ibid.*, § 85.
[34] *Ibid.*, §§ 74-80.
[35] *Ibid.*, § 84.

the Conclusion and could have been decisive factors in determination of the Appeals Chamber's remedies.[36]

22. The Prosecutor submits that the extreme measure of dismissal of the indictment with prejudice to the Prosecutor is not proportionate to the alleged violations of the Appellant's rights and is contrary to the mandate of the Tribunal to promote national reconciliation in Rwanda by conducting public trial on the merits.[37] She states that the Tribunal must take into account rules of law, the rights of the accused and particularly the interests of justice required by the victims and the international community as a whole.[38]

23. The Prosecutor alleges a violation of Rule 5, in that the Appeals Chamber exceeded its role and obtained facts which the Prosecutor alleges were outside the original trial record. The Prosecutor submits that in so doing the Appeals Chamber acted *ultra vires* the provisions of Rules 98, 115 and 117(A) with the result that the Prosecutor suffered material prejudice, the remedy for which is an order of the Appeals Chamber for review of the Decision, together with the accompanying Dispositive Orders.[39]

24. The Prosecutor submits that her ability to continue with prosecutions and investigations depends on the government of Rwanda and that, unless the Appellant is tried, the Rwandan government will no longer be "involved in any manner".[40]

25. Finally, the Prosecutor submits that review is justified on the basis of the new facts, which establish that the Prosecutor made significant efforts to transfer the Appellant, that the Prosecutor acted with due diligence and that any delays did not fundamentally compromise the rights of the Appellant and would not justify the dismissal of the indictment with prejudice to the Prosecutor.[41]

26. In terms of substantive relief, the Prosecutor requests that the Appeals Chamber either review the Decision or reconsider it in the exercise of its inherent powers, that it vacate the Decision and that it reinstate the Indictment. In the alternative, if these requests

[36] *Ibid.*, §§ 86,87.
[37] *Ibid.*, § 146.
[38] *Ibid.*, § 181.
[39] *Ibid.*, §§ 147-171.
[40] Transcript at pages 27 and 28.
[41] *Ibid.*, at page 122 and *supra* note 19 at § 184.

are not granted, the Prosecutor requests that the Decision dismissing the indictment is ordered to be without prejudice to the Prosecutor[42].

B. The Defence Case

27. The Appellant submits that Article 25 is only available to the parties after an accused has become a "convicted person". The Appeals Chamber does not have jurisdiction to consider the Prosecutor's Motion as the Appellant has not become a "convicted person" The Appellant submits that Rules 120 and 121 should be interpreted in accordance with this principle and maintains that both rules apply to review after trial and are therefore consistent with Article 25 which also applies to the right of review of a "convicted person"[43].

28. The Appellant submits that the Appeals Chamber does not have "inherent power" to revise a final decision. He submits that the Prosecutor is effectively asking the Appeals Chamber to amend the Statute by asking it to use its inherent power only if it concludes that Article 25 and Rule 120 do not apply. The Appellant states that the Appeals Chamber cannot on its own create law.[44]

29. The Appellant submits that the Decision was final and unappealable and that he should be released as there is no statutory authority to revise the Decision.[45]

30. The Appellant maintains that the Prosecutor has ignored the legal requirements for the introduction of new facts and has adduced no new facts to justify a review of the Decision. Despite the attachments provided by the Prosecutor and held out to be new facts, the Appellant submits that the Prosecutor has failed to produce any evidence to support the two-fold requirement in the Rules that the new fact should not have been known to the moving party and could not have been discovered through the exercise of due diligence.[46]

---

[42] *Supra* note 18 at § 7.
[43] *Appellant's Response to Prosecutor's Motion for Review or Reconsideration of the Appeals Chamber Decision rendered on 3 November 1999 in Jean-Bosco Barayagwiza v. The Prosecutor and Request for Stay of Execution* ("Appellant's Response") filed on 17th February 2000, at §§ 1-12. Transcript at page 129 *et seq.* and pages 227-230.
[44] Appellant's Response at §§ 13 – 16. Transcript at page 139 *et seq.*
[45] Appellant's Response at.§§ 17-24.
[46] *Ibid.*, § 28.

31. The Appellant submits that the Appeals Chamber should reject the request of the Prosecutor to classify the "old facts" as "new facts" as an attempt to invent a new definition limited to the facts of this case. The Appellant maintains that the Decision was correct in its findings and is fully supported by the Record.

32. The Appellant maintains that the Prosecutor's contention that the applicability of the abuse of process doctrine was not communicated to it before the Decision is groundless. The Appellant alleges that this issue was fully set out in his motion filed on 24 February 1998 and that when an issue has been properly raised by a party in criminal proceedings, the party who chooses to ignore the points raised by the other does so at its own peril.[47]

33. In relation to the submissions by the Prosecutor that the Decision of the Appeals Chamber was wrong in light of UN Resolution 955's goal of achieving national reconciliation for Rwanda, the Appellant urges the Appeals Chamber "to forcefully reject the notion that the human rights of a person accused of a serious crime, under the rubric of achieving national reconciliation, should be less than those available to an accused charged with a less serious one".[48]

[47] *Ibid.*, §§ 45-49.
[48] *Ibid.*, §§ 51-53.

V. THE MOTION BEFORE THE CHAMBER

34. Before proceeding to consider the Motion for Review, the Chamber notes that during the hearing on 22 February 2000 in Arusha, Prosecutor Ms Carla Del Ponte, made a statement regarding the reaction of the government of Rwanda to the Decision. She stated that: "The government of Rwanda reacted very seriously in a tough manner to the decision of 3 November 1999."[49] Later, the Attorney General of Rwanda appearing as representative of the Rwandan Government, in his submissions as "amicus curiae' to the Appeals Chamber, openly threatened the non co-operation of the peoples of Rwanda with the Tribunal if faced with an unfavourable Decision by the Appeals Chamber on the Motion for Review.[50] The Appeals Chamber wishes to stress that the Tribunal is an independent body. whose decisions are based solely on justice and law. If its decision in any case should be followed by non-cooperation, that consequence would be a matter for the Security Council.[51]

35. The Chamber notes also that, during the hearing on her Motion for Review, the Prosecutor based her arguments on the alleged guilt of the Appellant, and stated she was prepared to demonstrate this before the Chamber. The forcefulness with which she expressed her position compels us to reaffirm that it is for the Trial Chamber to adjudicate on the guilt of an accused, in accordance with the fundamental principle of the presumption of innocence, as incorporated in Article 3 of the Statute of the Tribunal.

36. The Motion for Review provides the Chamber with two alternative courses. First, it seeks a review of the Decision pursuant to Article 25 of said Statute. Further, failing this, it seeks that the Chamber reconsider the Decision by virtue of the power vested in it as a judicial body. We shall begin with the sought review.

---

[49] Transcript, pages 26-28.

[50] *Ibid*., pages 290 and 291 : The Attorney General representing the government of Rwanda referred to the "terrible consequences which a decision to release the appellant without a prospect of prosecution by this Tribunal or some other jurisdiction will give rise to. Such a decision will encourage impunity and hamper the efforts of Rwanda to maintain peace and stability and promote unity and reconciliation. A decision of this nature will cost the Tribunal heavily in terms of the support and goodwill of the people of Rwanda."

[51] Rule 7*bis* of the Rules. See also: Prosecutor v. Tihomir Blaškić, *Judgement on the Request of the Republic of Croatia for Review of the Decision of Trial Chamber II of 18 July 1997*, Case no. IT-95-14-AR108 bis. 29 October 1997 at §§ 26 and 33; Prosecutor v. Dusko Tadic, *Judgement*, Case no. IT-94-1-A, 15 July 1999 at §51.

A. REVIEW

1. General considerations

37. The mechanism provided in the Statute and Rules for application to a Chamber for review of a previous decision is not a novel concept invented specifically for the purposes of this Tribunal. In fact, it is a facility available both on an international level and indeed in many national jurisdictions, although often with differences in the criteria for a review to take place.

38. Article 61 of the Statute of the International Court of Justice is such a provision and provides the Court with the power to revise judgements on the discovery of a fact, of a decisive nature which was unknown to the court and party claiming revision when the judgement was given, provided this was not due to negligence [52]. Similarly Article 4 of Protocol No. 7 to the European Convention for the Protection of Human Rights and Fundamental Freedoms (1950) provides for the reopening of cases if there is *inter alia*, "evidence of new or newly discovered facts"[53]. Finally, on this subject, the International Law Commission has stated that such a provision was a "necessary guarantee against the possibility of factual error relating to material not available to the accused and therefore not brought to the attention of the Court at the time of the initial trial or of any appeal."[54]

39. In national jurisdictions, the facility for review exists in different forms, either specifically as a right to review a decision of a court, or by virtue of an alternative route which achieves the same result. Legislation providing a specific right to review is most prevalent in civil law jurisdictions, although again, the exact criteria to be fulfilled before a

---

[52] *Statute of the International Court of Justice as annexed to the Charter of the United Nations*. 26th June 1945, I.C.J. Acts and Documents No. 5 ("ICJ Statute"). See *Application for Revision and Interpretation of the Judgement of 24 February 1982 in the Case concerning the Continental Shelf (Tunisia/LibyanArab Jamahiriya)* 1985 (ICJ) Rep 192.

[53] 22 November 1984, 24 ILM 435 at 436.

[54] *Report of the International Law Commission on the work of its 46th session*. Official Records, 49th Session. Supplement number No.10 (A/49/10) at page 128. It should also be noted that the International Covenant on Civil and Political Rights (ICCPR) (1966) also refers to the discovery of "new or newly discovered facts" in Article 14. However it relates primarily to the right to compensation in the event that these new facts (together with other criteria) mean that a conviction is reversed or an accused pardoned.

court will undertake a review can differ from that provided in the legislation for this Tribunal[55].

40. These provisions are pointed out simply as being illustrative of the fact that, although the precise terms may differ, review of decisions is not a unique idea and the mechanism which has brought this matter once more before the Appeals Chamber is, in its origins, drawn from a variety of sources.

41. Returning to the procedure in hand, it is clear from the Statute and the Rules[56] that, in order for a Chamber to carry out a review, it must be satisfied that four criteria have been met. There must be a new fact; this new fact must not have been known by the moving party at the time of the original proceedings; the lack of discovery of the new fact must not have been through the lack of due diligence on the part of the moving party; and it must be shown that the new fact could have been a decisive factor in reaching the original decision.

42. The Appeals Chamber of the International Tribunal for the former Yugoslavia has highlighted the distinction, which should be made between genuinely new facts which may justify review and additional evidence of a fact [57]. In considering the application of Rule 119 of the Rules of the International Tribunal for the former Yugoslavia (which mirrors Rule 120 of the Rules), the Appeals Chamber held that:

> Where an applicant seeks to present a new fact which becomes known only after trial, despite the exercise of due diligence during the trial in discovering it, Rule 119 is the governing provision. In such a case, the Appellant is not seeking to admit additional evidence of a fact that was considered at trial but rather a new fact...It is for the Trial Chamber to review the Judgement and determine whether the new fact, if proved, could have been a decisive factor in reaching a decision".[58]

Further, the Appeals Chamber stated that-

[55] E.g. in Belgium-Article 443 *et seq.* of the Code d'Instruction Criminelle provides for "Demandes en Révision"; In Sweden, Chapter 58 of Part 7 of the Swedish Code of Judicial Procedure (which came into force on 1 January 1948, provision cited as per amendments of the Code as of 1 January 1999) provides for the right of review; In France, Article 622 *et seq.* of the Code de Procédure Pénale (as amended by the law of 23 June 1989) provides for "Demandes en Révision"; In Germany, Section 359 *et seq.* of the German Code of Criminal Procedure 1987 (as amended) provides for "re-opening"; In Italy, Articles 629-647 of the *Codice de Procedura Penale* provides for review; and in Spain Article 954 of *La Ley de Enjuiciamiento Criminal* provides for "Revision".
[56] Article 25, Rules 120 and 121.
[57] Prosecutor v. Duško Tadić, *Decision on Appellant's Motion for the extension of the time-limit and admission of additional evidence*, Case no, IT-94-1-A, 15th October 1998.
[58] *Ibid.*, at 30.

> a distinction exists between a fact and evidence of that fact. The mere subsequent discovery of evidence of a fact which was known at trial is not itself a new fact within the meaning of Rule 119 of the Rules.[59]

43. The Appeals Chamber would also point out at this stage, that although the substantive issue differed, in *Prosecutor v. Dražen Erdemović*,[60] the Appeals Chamber undertook to warn both parties that "[t]he appeal process of the International Tribunal is not designed for the purpose of allowing parties to remedy their own failings or oversights during trial or sentencing". The Appeals Chamber confirms that it notes and adopts both this observation and the test established in *Prosecutor v. Duško Tadić* in consideration of the matter before it now.

44. The Appeals Chamber notes the submissions made by both parties on the criteria, and the differences which emerge. In particular it notes the fact that the Prosecutor places the new facts she submits into two categories (paragraph 15 above), the Appellant in turn asking the Appeals Chamber to reject this submission as an attempt by the Prosecutor to classify "old facts" as "new facts" (paragraph 31 above). In considering the "new facts" submitted by the Prosecutor, the Appeals Chamber applies the test outlined above and confirms that it considers, as was submitted by the Prosecutor, that a "new fact" cannot be considered as failing to satisfy the criteria simply because it occurred before the trial. What is crucial is satisfaction of the criteria which the Appeals Chamber has established will apply. If a "new" fact satisfies these criteria, and could have been a decisive factor in reaching the decision, the Appeals Chamber can review the Decision.

2. Admissibility

45. The Appellant pleads that the Prosecutor's Motion for Review is inadmissible, because by virtue of Article 25 of the Statute only the Prosecutor or a convicted person may seise the Tribunal with a motion for review of the sentence. In the Appellant's view, the reference to a convicted person means that this article applies only after a conviction has been delivered. According to the counsel of the Appellant:

> Rule 120 of the Rules of Procedure and Evidence is not intended for revision or review before conviction, but after ... a proper trial.[61]

---

[59] *Ibid.*, at 32.

[60] *Judgement*, Case no IT-96-22-A, 7 October 1997 at § 15.

[61] Transcript of the hearing of 22 February 2000 ("transcript"), p.134.

As there was no trial in this case, there is no basis for seeking a review.

46. The Prosecutor responds that the reference to "the convicted person or the Prosecutor" in the said article serves solely to spell out that either of the two parties may seek review, not that there must have been a conviction before the article could apply. If a decision could be reviewed only following a conviction, no injustice stemming from an unwarranted acquittal could ever be redressed. In support of her interpretation, the Prosecutor compares Article 25 with Article 24, which also refers to persons convicted and to the Prosecutor being entitled to lodge appeals. She argued that it was common ground that the Prosecutor could appeal against a decision of acquittal, which would not be the case if the interpretation submitted by the Appellant was accepted.

47. Both Article 24 (which relates to appellate proceedings) and Article 25 of the Statute, expressly refer to a convicted person. However, Rule 72D and consistent decisions of both Tribunals [62] demonstrate that a right of appeal is also available in *inter alia* the case of dismissal of preliminary motions brought before a Trial Chamber, which raised an objection based on lack of jurisdiction.[63] Such appeals are on interlocutory matters and therefore by definition do not involve a remedy available only following conviction. Accordingly, it is the Appeals Chamber's view that the intention was not to interpret the Rules restrictively in the sense suggested by the Appellant, such that availability of the right to apply for review is only triggered on conviction of the accused; the Appeals Chamber will not accept the narrow interpretation of the Rules submitted by the Appellant. If the Appellant were correct that there could be no review unless there has been a conviction, it would follow that there could be no appeal from acquittal for the same reason. Appeals from acquittals have been allowed before the Appeals Chamber of the ICTY. The Appellant's logic is not therefore correct. Furthermore, in this case, the Appellant himself had recourse to the mechanism of interlocutory appeals which would not have been successful had the Chamber accepted the arguments he is now putting forward.

48. The Appeals Chamber accordingly subscribes to the Prosecutor's reasoning. Inclusion of the reference to the "Prosecutor" and the " convicted person" in the wording of

[62] i.e. the International Tribunal for the Former Yugoslavia (ICTY) and the International Criminal Tribunal for Rwanda (ICTR).

[63] Rule 72(D) of the Rules. See also the additional provisions for appeal provided in Rules 65(D), 77D and 91(C) of the Rules, and in Rules 72, 73, 77(J), 65(D), 91(C) of the Rules of Procedure and Evidence of the ICTY, as pointed out in the Reply at §§ 11.

the article indicates that each of the parties may seek review of a decision, not that the provision is to apply only after a conviction has been delivered.

49. The Chamber considers it important to note that only a final judgement may be reviewed pursuant to Article 25 of the Statute and to Rule 120[64]. The parties submitted pleadings on the final or non-final nature of the Decision in connection with the request for reconsideration. The Chamber would point out that a final judgement in the sense of the above-mentioned articles is one which terminates the proceedings; only such a decision may be subject to review. Clearly, the Decision of 3 November 1999 belongs to that category, since it dismissed the indictment against the Appellant and terminated the proceedings.

50. The Appeals Chamber therefore has jurisdiction to review its Decision pursuant to Article 25 of the Statute and to Rule 120.

3. Merits

51. With respect to this Motion for Review, the Appeals Chamber begins by confirming its Decision of 3 November 1999 on the basis of the facts it was founded on. As a judgement by the Appeals Chamber, the Decision may be altered only if new facts are discovered which were not known at the time of the trial or appeal proceedings and which could have been a decisive factor in the decision. Pursuant to Article 25 of the Statute, in such an event the parties may submit to the Tribunal an application for review of the judgement, as in the instant case before the Chamber.

52. The Appeals Chamber confirms that in considering the facts submitted to it by the Prosecutor as "new facts", it applies the criteria drawn from the relevant provisions of the Statute and Rules as laid down above. The Chamber considers first whether the Prosecutor submitted new facts which were not known at the time of the proceedings before the Chamber, and which could have been a decisive factor in the decision, pursuant to Article 25 of the Statute. It then considers the condition introduced by Rule 120, that the new facts not be known to the party concerned or not be discoverable due diligence notwithstanding. If the Chamber is satisfied, it accordingly reviews its decision in the light of such new facts.

[64] In this respect, the Appeals Chamber does not agree with the *Decision on the Alternative Request for Renewed Consideration of Delalić's Motion for an Adjournment until 22 June or Request for Issue of Subpoenas to Individuals and Requests for Assistance to the Government of Bosnia and Herzegovina* (IT-96-

53. In considering these issues, the Appellant's detention may be divided into three periods. The first, namely the period where the Appellant was subject to the extradition procedure, starts with his arrest by the Cameroonian authorities on 15 April 1996 and ends on 21 February 1997 with the decision of the Court of Appeal of the Centre of Cameroon rejecting the request for extradition from the Rwandan government. The second, the period relating to the transfer decision, runs from the Rule 40 request for the Appellant's provisional detention, through his transfer to the Tribunal's detention unit on 19 November 1997. The third period begins with the arrival of the Appellant at the detention unit on 19 November 1997 and ends with his initial appearance on 23 February 1998.

(a) First period (15.4.1996 – 21.2.1997)

54. The Appeals Chamber considers that several elements submitted by the Prosecutor in support of her Motion for Review are evidence rather than facts. The elements presented in relation to the first period consist of transcripts of proceedings before the Cameroonian courts: on 28 March 1996 ; 29 March 1996 ; 17 April 1996 and 3 May 1996.[65] It is manifest from the transcript of 3 May 1996 that the Tribunal's request was discussed[66] at that hearing. The Appellant addressed the court and opposed Rwanda's request for extradition, stating that, « c'est le tribunal international qui est compétent »[67]. The Appeals Chamber considers that it may accordingly be presumed that the Appellant was informed of the nature of the crimes he was wanted for by the Prosecutor. This was a new fact for the Appeals Chamber. The Decision is based on the fact that:

> l'Appelant a été détenu pendant une durée totale de 11 mois avant d'être informé de la nature générale des chefs d'accusation que le Procureur avait retenus contre lui. [68]

The information now before the Chamber demonstrates that, on the contrary, the Appellant knew the general nature of the charges against him by 3 May 1996 at the latest. He thus spent at most 18 days in detention without being informed of the reasons therefor.

21-T, 22 June 1998), *which suggests that interlocutory decisions can be subject to review*. The Appeals Chamber confirms that the law is as stated above.

[65] Annexes 8, 9 and 11 to the Motion for Review.

[66] On page 3 of the transcript of 3 May, the Public Prosecutor explains that he is waiting for "the Tribunal to send us the relevant documentation (« *que le Tribunal International nous procure les documents* »).

55. The Appeals Chamber considers that such a time period violates the Appellant's right to be informed without delay of the charges against him. However, this violation is patently of a different order than the one identified in the Decision whereby the Appellant was without any information for 11 months.

(b) <u>Second period (21.2.1997 – 19.11.1997)</u>

56. With respect to the second period, the one relative to the transfer decision, several elements are submitted to the Chamber's scrutiny as new facts. They consist of Annexes 1 to 7, 10 and 12 to the Motion for Review. The Chamber considers the following to be material:

1. The report by Judge Mballe of the Supreme Court of Cameroon.[69] In his report, Justice Mballe explains that the request by the Prosecutor pursuant to Article 40 *bis* was transmitted immediately to the President of the Republic for him to sign a legislative decree authorising the accused's transfer. As he sees it, if the legislative decree could be signed only on 21 October 1997 that was due to the pressure exerted by the Rwandan authorities on Cameroon for the extradition of detainees to Kigali. He adds that in any event this semi-political semi-judicial extradition procedure was not the one that should have been followed.

2. A statement by David Scheffer, ambassador-at-large for war crimes issues, of the United States.[70] Mr. Scheffer described his involvement in the Appellant's case between September and November 1997. In his statement, Mr. Scheffer explains that the signing of the Presidential legislative decree was delayed owing to the elections scheduled for October 1997, and that Mr. Bernard Muna of the Prosecutor's Office asked Mr. Scheffer to intervene to speed up the transfer. He went on to say that, subsequent to that request, the United States Embassy made several representations to the Government of Cameroon in this regard between September and November 1997. Mr. Scheffer says he also wrote to the Government on 13 September 1997 and that around 24 October 1997

---

[67] Page 4 of the transcript.
[68] Decision, §85.
[69] Annexe N°1 de la Demande en révision.
[70] Filed on 10 December 1999.

the Cameroonian authorities notified the United States Embassy of their willingness to effect the transfer.

57. In the Appeals Chamber's view a relevant new fact emerges from this information. In its Decision, the Chamber determined on the basis of the evidence adduced at the time that "Cameroon was willing to transfer the Appellant"[71], as there was no proof to the contrary. The above information however goes to show that Cameroon had not been prepared to effect its transfer before 24 October 1997. This fact is new. The request pursuant to Article 40 bis had been wrongly subject to an extradition process, when under Article 28 of the Statute all States had an obligation to co-operate with the Tribunal. The President of Cameroon had elections forthcoming, which could not prompt him to accede to such a request. And it was the involvement of the United States, in the person of Mr. Scheffer, which in the end led to the transfer.

58. The new fact, that Cameroon was not prepared to transfer the Appellant prior to the date on which he was actually delivered to the Tribunal's detention unit, would have had a significant impact on the Decision had it been known at the time, given that, in the Decision, the Appeals Chamber drew its conclusions with regard to the Prosecutor's negligence in part from the fact that nothing prevented the transfer of the Appellant save the Prosecutor's failure to act:

> It is also clear from the record that the Prosecutor made no efforts to have the Appellant transferred to the Tribunal's detention unit until after he filed the *writ of habeas corpus*. **Similarly, the Prosecutor has made no showing that such efforts would have been futile. There is nothing in the record that indicates that Cameroon was not willing to transfer the Appellant.** Rather it appears that the Appellant was simply forgotten about.[72]

The Appeals Chamber considered that the human rights of the Appellant were violated by the Prosecutor during his detention in Cameroon. However, the new facts show that, during this second period, the violations were not attributable to the Prosecutor.

(c) <u>Third period (19.11.1997 – 23.2.1998)</u>

59. In her Motion for Review, the Prosecutor submitted few elements relating to the third period, that is the detention in Arusha. However, on 16 February 2000 she lodged

[71] Decision, §59.
[72] Decision, §96 (emphasis added).

additional material in this regard, along with a motion for deferring the time-limits imposed for her to submit new facts. Having examined the Prosecutor's request and the Registrar's memorandum relative thereto as well as the Appellant's written response lodged on 28 February 2000[73], the Appeals Chamber decides to accept this additional information.

60. The material submitted by the Prosecutor consists of a letter to the Registrar dated 11 February 2000, and annexes thereto. A relevant fact emerges from it. The letter and its annexes indicate that Mr. Nyaberi, counsel for the defence, entered into talks with the Registrar in order to set a date for the initial appearance. Several provisional dates were discussed. Problems arose with regard to the availability of judges and of defence counsel. Annex C to the Registrar's letter indicates that Mr. Nyaberi assented to the initial appearance taking place on 3 February 1997. This was not challenged by the defence at the hearing.

61. The assent of the defence counsel to deferring the initial appearance until 3 February 1997 is a new fact for the Appeals Chamber. During the proceedings before the Chamber, only the judicial recess was offered by way of explanation for the 96-day period which elapsed between the Appellant's transfer and his initial appearance, and this was rejected by the Chamber. There was no suggestion whatsoever that the Appellant had assented to any part of that schedule.

> There is no evidence that the Appellant was afforded an opportunity to appear before an independent Judge during the period of the provisional detention and the Appellant contends that he was denied this opportunity.[74]

62. The decision by the Appeals Chamber in respect of the period of detention in Arusha is based on a 96-day lapse between the Appellant's transfer and his initial appearance. The new fact relative hereto, the defence counsel's agreeing to a hearing being held on 3 February 1997, reduces that lapse to 20 days - from 3 to 23 February. The Chamber considers that this is still a substantial delay and that the Appellant's rights have still been violated. However, the Appeals Chamber finds that the period during which these violations took place is less extensive than it appeared at the time of the Decision.

[73] The President of the Appeals Chamber authorised the filing of this document during the hearing of 22 February, see page 57 of the transcript.
[74] Decision, §69.

(d) <u>Were the new facts known to the Prosecutor?</u>

63. Rule 120 introduces a condition which is not stated in Article 25 of the Statute which addresses motions for review. According to Rule 120 a party may submit a motion for review to the Chamber only if the new fact "was not known **to the moving party** at the time of the proceedings before a Chamber, **and could not have been discovered through the exercise of due diligence**" (emphasis added).

64. The new facts identified in the first two periods were not known to the Chamber at the time of its Decision but they may have been known to the Prosecutor or at least they could have been discovered. With respect to the second period, the Prosecutor was not unaware that Cameroon was unwilling to transfer the Appellant, especially as it was her deputy, Mr. Muna, who sought Mr. Scheffer's intervention to facilitate the process. But evidently it was not known to the Chamber at the time of the Appeal proceedings. On the contrary, the elements before the Chamber led it to the opposite finding, which was an important factor in its conclusion that "the Prosecutor has failed with respect to her obligation to prosecute the case with due diligence."[75]

65. In the wholly exceptional circumstances of this case, and in the face of a possible miscarriage of justice, the Chamber construes the condition laid down in Rule 120, that the fact be unknown to the moving party at the time of the proceedings before a Chamber, and not discoverable through the exercise of due diligence, as directory in nature. In adopting such a position, the Chamber has regard to the circumstance that the Statute itself does not speak to this issue.

66. There is precedent for taking such an approach. Other reviewing courts, presented with facts which would clearly have altered an earlier decision, have felt bound by the interests of justice to take these into account, even when the usual requirements of due diligence and unavailability were not strictly satisfied. While it is not in the interests of justice that parties be encouraged to proceed in a less than diligent manner, "courts cannot close their eyes to injustice on account of the facility of abuse"[76].

---

[75] Decision, §101.
[76] Berggren v Mutual Life Insurance Co., 231 Mass. at 177. The full passage reads:
"The mischief naturally flowing from retrials based upon the discovery of alleged new evidence leads to the establishment of a somewhat stringent practice against granting such motions unless upon a survey of the

67. The Court of Appeal of England and Wales had to consider a situation not unlike that currently before the Appeals Chamber in the matter of *Hunt and Another v Atkin*.[77] In that case, a punitive order was made against a firm of solicitors for having taken a certain course of action. It emerged that the solicitors were in possession of information that justified their actions to a certain extent, and which they had failed to produce on an earlier occasion, despite enquiries from the court. As in the current matter, the moving party (the solicitors) claimed that the court's enquiries had been unclear, and that they had not fully understood the nature of the evidence to be presented. The Judge approached the question as follows:

> I hope I can be forgiven for taking a very simplistic view of this situation. What I think I have to ask myself is this: if these solicitors ... had produced a proper affidavit on the last occasion containing the information which is now given to me ...would I have made the order in relation to costs that I did make? It is a very simplistic approach, but I think it is probably necessary in this situation.

He concluded that he would not have made the same order, and so allowed the fresh evidence and ordered a retrial. The Court of Appeal upheld his decision.

68. Faced with a similar problem, the Supreme Court of Canada has held that the requirements of due diligence and unavailability are to be applied less strictly in criminal than in civil cases. In the leading case of *McMartin v The Queen*, the court held, *per* Ritchie J, that:

> In all the circumstance, if the evidence is considered to be of sufficient strength that it might reasonably affect the verdict of the jury, I do not think it should be excluded on the ground that reasonable diligence was not exercised to obtain it at or before the trial.[78]

69. The Appeals Chamber does not cite these examples as authority for its actions in the strict sense. The International Tribunal is a unique institution, governed by its own Statute and by the provisions of customary international law, where these can be discerned. However, the Chamber notes that the problems posed by the Request for Review have been considered ~~by other~~ jurisdictions, and that the approach adopted by the Appeals Chamber here is not unfamiliar to those separate and independent systems. To reject the facts

---

whole case a miscarriage of justice is likely to result if a new trial is denied. This is the fundamental test, in aid of which most if not all the rules upon the matter from time to time alluded to have been formulated. Ease in obtaining new trials would offer temptations to the securing of fresh evidence to supply former deficiencies. But courts cannot close their eyes to injustice on account of facility of abuse'."

[77] Court of Appeal (Civil Division) 6 May 1964.

presented by the Prosecutor, in the light of their impact on the Decision, would indeed be to close ones eyes to reality.

70. With regard to the third period, the Appeals Chamber remarks that, although a set of the elements submitted by the Prosecutor on 16 February 2000 were available to her prior to that date, according to the Registrar's memorandum, Annex C was not one of them. It must be deduced that the fact that the defence counsel had given his consent was known to the Prosecutor at the time of the proceedings before the Appeals Chamber.

4. Conclusion

71. The Chamber notes that the remedy it ordered for the violations the Appellant was subject to is based on a cumulation of elements:

> ... the fundamental rights of the Appellant were repeatedly violated. What may be worse, it appears that the Prosecutor's failure to prosecute this case was tantamount to negligence. We find this conduct to be egregious and, in light of the numerous violations, conclude that the only remedy for such prosecutorial inaction and the resultant denial of his rights is to release the Appellant and dismiss the charges against him.[79]

The new facts diminish the role played by the failings of the Prosecutor as well as the intensity of the violation of the rights of the Appellant. The cumulative effect of these elements being thus reduced, the reparation ordered by the Appeals Chamber now appears disproportionate in relation to the events. The new facts being therefore facts which could have been decisive in the Decision, in particular as regards the remedy it orders, that remedy must be modified.

72. The Prosecutor has submitted that it has suffered "material prejudice" from the non compliance by the Appeals Chamber with the Rules and that consequently it is entitled to relief as provided in Rule 5. As the Appeals Chamber believes that this issue is not relevant to the Motion for Review and as the Appeals Chamber has in any event decided to review its Decision, it will not consider this issue further.

---

[78] (1964) 1 CCC 142, 46 DLR (2d) 372.
[79] Decision, §106.

B. RECONSIDERATION

73. The essential basis on which the Prosecutor sought a reconsideration of the previous Decision, as distinguished from a review, was that she was not given a proper hearing on the issues passed on in that Decision. The Appeals Chamber finds no merit in the contention and accordingly rejects the request for reconsideration.

VI. CONCLUSION

74. The Appeals Chamber reviews its Decision in the light of the new facts presented by the Prosecutor. It confirms that the Appellant's rights were violated, and that all violations demand a remedy. However, the violations suffered by the Appellant and the omissions of the Prosecutor are not the same as those which emerged from the facts on which the Decision is founded. Accordingly, the remedy ordered by the Chamber in the Decision, which consisted in the dismissal of the indictment and the release of the Appellant, must be altered.

VII. DISPOSITION

75. For these reasons, the APPEALS CHAMBER reviews its Decision of 3 November 1999 and replaces its Disposition with the following:

1) ALLOWS the Appeal having regard to the violation of the rights of the Appellant to the extent indicated above;

2) REJECTS the application by the Appellant to be released;

3) DECIDES that for the violation of his rights the Appellant is entitled to a remedy, to be fixed at the time of judgement at first instance, as follows:

    a) If the Appellant is found not guilty, he shall receive financial compensation;

    b) If the Appellant is found guilty, his sentence shall be reduced to take account of the violation of his rights.

Judge Vohrah and Judge Nieto-Navia append Declarations to this Decision.

Judge Shahabuddeen appends a Separate Opinion to this Decision.

Done in both English and French, the French text being authoritative.

s/.	s/.	s/.
Claude Jorda, Presiding	Lal Chand Vohrah	Mohamed Shahabuddeen

s/.	s/.
Rafael Nieto-Navia	Fausto Pocar

Dated this thirty-first day of March 2000
At The Hague,
The Netherlands

[Seal of the Tribunal]

DECLARATION OF JUDGE LAL CHAND VOHRAH

1. I would like to reiterate that I fully agree with the conclusions of the Appeals Chamber in the present decision and with the disposition that follows this Review. This agreement, however, calls for a few observations on my part. In the original decision the Appeals Chamber invoked the abuse of process doctrine. In the light of the facts which where then before it, the Chamber found that to proceed with the trial of the Appellant in the face of the egregious violations of his rights would be unjust to him and injurious to the integrity of the judicial process of the Tribunal. Consequently, the Appeals Chamber decided that the proceedings against the Appellant should be discontinued.

2. In its previous decision, the Appeals Chamber proceeded on the basis of, *inter alia*, its finding that the Prosecutor was responsible for the delays of which the Appellant complained. In this Review a different picture has been shown by the disclosure of new facts which now diminish substantially the blameworthiness attributed to the Prosecutor on the ground of lack of diligence, and the seriousness of the violations suffered by the Appellant. Had the Appeals Chamber been apprised of these facts on appeal, the original decision would have been different and the abuse of process doctrine would not have been called in aid and applied with all the vigour that was implicit in the "with prejudice" order that was made.

3. I must say that I have had the benefit of reading the Declaration in draft of my brother Judge Nieto-Navia and would like to state that I subscribe fully to the views he has expressed therein on the overriding principle relating to the independence of the judiciary (in the light of the considerations which the Prosecutor and the Representative of the Government of Rwanda as amicus curiae have, perhaps unwittingly, asked the Appeals Chamber to take into account), and on the principles of human rights.

4. In conclusion, I am satisfied that there are new facts which now require that the previous decision be modified in the way stated in the disposition of the present decision.

Done in English and French, the English text being authoritative.

S/.

Lal Chand Vohrah

Dated this 31st day of March 2000
At The Hague,
The Netherlands.

[Seal of the Tribunal]

DECLARATION OF JUDGE RAFAEL NIETO-NAVIA

1. It is necessary to consider the role of the Tribunal in the context of its mandate in Rwanda as dispenser of justice and the effect, if any, of politics on its work in prosecuting those responsible for genocide and other serious violations of international humanitarian law.

2. This issue was raised specifically during the oral hearing on this matter, in Arusha, on 22 February 2000 by the Chief Prosecutor. It is expedient to set out the relevant section:

> "Let me just say a few words with respect to the government of Rwanda. The government of Rwanda reacted very seriously in a tough manner to the decision of 3 November 1999. It was a politically motivated decision, which is understandable. It can only be understood if one is cognisant with the situation, if one is aware of what happened in Rwanda in 1994. I also notice that, well, it was the Prosecutor that had no visa to travel to Rwanda. It was the Prosecutor who was unable to go to her office in Kigali. It was the Prosecutor who could not be received by the Rwandan authorities. In November, after your decision, there was no co-operation, no collaboration with the office of the Prosecutor. In other words, justice, as dispensed by this Tribunal was paralysed. It was the trial of Baglishima which had to be adjourned because the Rwandan government did not allow 16 witnesses to appear before this Court. In other words, they were not allowed to leave the territory of Rwanda. Fortunately, things have improved currently, and we again enjoy the support of the government. Why? Because we were able to show our good will, our willingness to continue with our work based on the mandate entrusted to us. However, your Honours, due account has to be taken of that fact. Whether we want it or not, we must come to terms with the fact that our ability to continue with our prosecution and investigations depend on the government of Rwanda. That is the reality that we face. What is the reality? Either Barayagwiza can be tried by this Tribunal, in the alternative; or the only other solution that you have is for Barayagwiza to be handed over to the state of Rwanda to his natural judge, judex naturalis. Otherwise I am afraid, as we say in Italian, possiamo chiudere la baracca. In other words we can as well put the key to that door, close the door and then open that of the prison. And in that case the Rwandan government will not be involved in any manner"[1]

3. The Prosecutor maintained that after the Decision in the instant case was rendered by the Appeals Chamber on 3 November 1999 (hereinafter "the Decision"), justice before the International Criminal Tribunal for Rwanda was effectively suspended as a result of action taken by the Rwandan government, who reacted essentially to what they viewed as an adverse decision of the Appeals Chamber.

[1] Transcript of the hearing on 22 February 2000, (the 'Transcript'), pp. 26-28.

4. It would be naïve to assert that the Tribunal does not depend on the co-operation of States for it to fulfil its duties. Indeed the Appeals Chamber itself has held that

> "The International Tribunal must turn to States if it is effectively to investigate crimes, collect evidence, summon witnesses and have indictees arrested and surrendered to the International Tribunal."[2]

Without State co-operation, the work of the Tribunal would be rendered impossible.

5. In order to cater for this, and aware of the need to ensure effective and ongoing co-operation, Article 28 of the Statute compels States to co-operate with the Tribunal "in the investigation and prosecution of persons accused of committing serious violations of international humanitarian law"[3]. This is a general obligation incumbent on all States but the Rwandan government is specially obliged, because the Tribunal was established "for the sole purpose of prosecuting persons responsible for genocide and other serious violations of International Humanitarian Law committed in the territory of Rwanda"[4]. In addition, being the territory in which most of the crimes alleged took place, the co-operation of the Rwandan government with the Tribunal in fulfilment of their obligations as prescribed by Article 28, is paramount.

6. This obligation of the Rwandan government is absolute. It is an obligation which cannot be overridden in particular circumstances by considerations of convenience or politics.

7. In my view, the Appeals Chamber, although mindful of this essential need for co-operation by the Rwandan government, is also mindful of the role the Tribunal plays in this process and therefore I refute most strenuously the suggestion that in reaching decisions, political considerations should play a persuasive or governing role, in order to assuage States and ensure co-operation to achieve the long-term goals of the Tribunal. On the contrary, in no circumstances would such considerations cause the Tribunal to compromise

---

[2] Prosecutor v. Tihomir Blaškić, *Judgement on the Request of the Republic of Croatia for Review of the Decision of Trial Chamber II of 18 July 1997*, Case no. IT-95-14-*AR108bis*, 29 October 1997, §26.

[3] Article 28.1. *Security Council Resolution 955 (1994) (S/RES/955) (1994)* § 2, also states that "all states shall cooperate fully with the International Tribunal and its organs in accordance with the present resolution and the Statute of the International Tribunal and that consequently all States shall take any measures necessary under their domestic law to implement the provisions of the present resolution and the Statute, including the obligation of States to comply with requests for assistance or orders issued by a Trial Chaber under Article 28 of the Statute, and requests States to keep the Secretary-General informed of such measures."

its judicial independence and integrity. This is a Tribunal whose decisions must be taken, solely with the intention of both implementing the law and guaranteeing justice to the case before it, not as a result of political pressure and threats to withhold co-operation being exerted by an angry government.

8. Faced with non co-operation by a State and having exhausted the facilities available to it to ensure co-operation, a clear mechanism has been provided in the Statute and Rules[5] whereby the Tribunal may make a finding concerning the particular State's failure to observe the provisions of the Statute or the Rules and thereafter may report this finding to the Security Council.[6] It then falls to the Security Council to determine appropriate action to take against the State in question.[7] The involvement of the Tribunal will cease at the point of referral to the Security Council and indeed its position is safeguarded further by the stipulation, as has been held, that "the finding by the International Tribunal must not include any recommendations or suggestions as to the course of action the Security Council may wish to take as a consequence of that finding."[8]. This mechanism ensures that clear separation in roles is maintained and more importantly that the independence of the Tribunal cannot be called into question. Its mandate is the prosecution of those responsible for serious violations of international humanitarian law[9] and it must do so in an impartial and unbiased fashion. It must not qualify this independence under any circumstances.

9. The concept of "the separation of powers" plays a central role in national jurisdictions. This concept ensures that a clear division is maintained between the functions of the legislature, judiciary and executive and provides that "one branch is not permitted to encroach on the domain or exercise the powers of another branch." [10] It ensures that the judiciary maintains a role apart from political considerations and safeguards its independence.

---

[4] *Security Council Resolution 955 (1994) (S/RES/955)(1994)* § 1.
[5] *E.g.*, Rule 54 includes the power to issue orders, summonses, subpoenas, warrants and transfer orders. *See* Prosecutor v. Duško Tadić, *Judgement*, Case no. IT-94-1-A, 15 July 1999, § 52.
[6] Rule *7bis* of the Rules. *Supra* note 2 at 26 and 33. Also, Prosecutor v. Duško Tadić, *Judgement*, Case no. IT-94-1-A, 15 July 1999 § 51.
[7] Such failure by States to comply with their obligations under the Statute, have been referred to the Security Council on several occasions to date *(Supra.* note 2, § 34).
[8] *Supra.* note 2 § 36.
[9] Article 1 of the Statute.
[10] *Blacks Law Dictionary*, 6th edition, West Publishing Co, 1990, p. 1365.

10. As a result, the judiciary holds a privileged position in national jurisdictions and is subjected to unceasing public scrutiny of its activities. This however is accepted as being a necessary component of its existence so that public confidence in the system can be maintained.

11. In consideration of this issue, I note the importance accorded to the principle by the United Nations, in appointing a Special Rapporteur on the Independence of Judges and Lawyers and by the General Assembly, in the promulgation of the 1985 UN Basic Principles on the Independence of the Judiciary.[11] The Principles as a whole are of the utmost importance, but it serves now to highlight the following provisions:

> "1. The independence of the judiciary shall be guaranteed by the State and enshrined in the Constitution or the laws of the country. It is the duty of all government and other institutions to respect and observe the independence of the judiciary;
>
> 2. The judiciary shall decide matters before it impartially, on the basis of facts and in accordance with the law, without any restrictions, improper influences, inducements, pressures, threats or interferences, direct or indirect, from any quarter or for any reason.[12]"

The principle of the independence of the judiciary is overriding and should at all times take precedence faced with any conflict, political pressures or interference. The proposition put forward by the Prosecutor that political considerations can play a role in the Appeals Chamber's decision making and actions is not acceptable.

12. Indeed it is important to note the remark made by Robert H. Jackson, Chief of Counsel for the United States at the International Military Tribunal, sitting at Nuremberg, in his opening speech before the Tribunal on 21 November 1945:

[11] *Seventh United Nations Congress on the Prevention of Crime and the Treatment of Offenders*, Milan, 26 August - 6 September 1985: Report prepared by the Secretariat Chap.IV, sect. B, as referred to in GA Resolution A/RES/40/146 of 13 December 1985 "*Human Rights in the Administration of Justice*". The Resolution was also pointed out by the Appellant in the Oral Hearing on 22 February 2000 and recorded at page 213 of the Transcript.

[12] *Ibid.*, § 1, 2. Note also, the UN 1990 Basic Principles on the Role of Lawyers adopted by the Eighth United Nations Congress on the Prevention of Crime and the Treatment of Offenders, at its meeting in Havana, Cuba from 27 August to 7 September 1990. The General Assembly has welcomed these principles and invites governments to respect them and to take them into account within the framework of their national legislation and practice (A/RES/45/166 of 18 December 1990).

> "The United States believed that the law has long afforded standards by which a juridical hearing could be conducted to make sure that we punish only the right men and for the right reasons"[13]

13. Political reasons are not the right reasons. The Tribunal is endowed with a Statute, which ensures that trials take place by means of a transparent process, wherein widely accepted international standards of criminal law are applied. Central to this process is the maintenance of human rights standards of the highest level, to ensure that the basic Rule of Law is upheld.

14. The basic human right of an accused to be tried before an independent and impartial tribunal is recognised also in the major human rights treaties and is one to which the Tribunal accords the utmost importance.[14] Indeed the Appeals Chamber in a case before the ICTY, held in consideration of its function that:

> "For a Tribunal such as this one to be established according to the rule of law, it must be established in accordance with the proper international standards; it must provide all the guarantees of fairness, justice and even-handedness, in full conformity with internationally recognised human rights instruments"[15]

15. It must not be forgotten that the Rwandan government itself has recognised the importance of impartial justice. In requesting the establishment of a Tribunal by the international community, the Rwandan government stated that it supported an international tribunal because of its desire to avoid "any suspicion of its wanting to organise speedy vengeful justice".[16] Accordingly, this Tribunal's fundamental aim is to vindicate the highest standards of international criminal justice, in providing an impartial and equitable system of justice.

---

[13] *The Trial of German Major War Criminals by the International Military Tribunal sitting at Nuremberg Germany (commencing 20 November 1945) Opening Speeches of the Chief Prosecutors.* Published under the Authority of H.M. Attorney-General By His Majesty's Stationery Office, London: 1946. pp. 36 and 37.

[14] Article 14 (1) of the *International Covenant of Civil and Political Rights, 1966* ("ICCPR") provides, *inter alia*, that "everyone shall be entitled to a fair and public hearing by a competent, independent and impartial tribunal established by law". Similarly, Article 6(1) of the *European Convention for the Protection of Human Rights and Fundamental Freedoms* (1950) ("ECHR"), protects the right to a fair trial and requires, *inter alia*, that cases be heard by an "independent and impartial tribunal established by law," and Article 8(1) of the *American Convention on Human Rights* (1969) ("ACHR") provides that "[e]very person has the right to a hearing, with due guarantees and within a reasonable time, by a competent, independent and impartial tribunal, previously established by law."

[15] Prosecutor v. Duško Tadić, *Decision on the Defence Motion for Interlocutory Appeal on Jurisdiction*, Case no. IT-94-1-AR72, 2 October 1995, § 45.

[16] UN Doc. S/PV.3453 (1994) at 14.

16. But now the government of Rwanda has suggested that the Tribunal should convict all the indictees who come before it. It is wrong. The accused can be acquitted if the Trial Chamber is not satisfied that guilt has been proven beyond a reasonable doubt.[17] Alternatively, the accused can be released on procedural grounds, as was the case in the Decision. In the application of impartial justice the role of the Tribunal is not simply to convict all those who appear before it, but to consider a case upholding the fundamental principles of human rights.

17. By virtue of Resolution 955 of 1994, the Security Council stated:

> "Convinced that in the particular circumstances of Rwanda, the prosecution of persons responsible for serious violations of international humanitarian law would enable this aim to be achieved and would contribute to the process of national reconciliation and to the restoration and maintenance of peace",[18]

This was subsequently reiterated by Resolution 1165 of 1998, when the Security Council stated that it "remain[ed] convinced that in the particular circumstances of Rwanda, the prosecution of persons responsible for serious violations of international humanitarian law will contribute to the process of national reconciliation and to the restoration and maintenance of peace in Rwanda and in the region"[19]. This aim can only be achieved by an independent Tribunal, mindful of the task entrusted to it by the international community.

18. Both Tribunals, ICTY and ICTR, find themselves in the midst of very emotive atmospheres and are charged with the duty to maintain their independence and transparency, as expected by the international community, preserving the norms of international human rights. The international community needs to be sure that justice is being served but that it is being served through the application of their Rules and Statutes, which are applied in a consistent and unbiased manner. I recall the words of the Zimbabwean Court in the Mlambo case, as cited in the Decision:

> "The charges against the applicant are far from trivial and there can be no doubt that it would be in the best interests of society to proceed with the trial of those who are

[17] Rule 87(A) of the Rules of Procedure and Evidence.
[18] *Supra* note 4.
[19] *Security Council Resolution 1165 (1998) (S/RES/1165) (1998).*

> charged with the commission of serious crimes. Yet that trial can only be undertaken if the guarantee under.... the Constitution has not been infringed."[20]

Difficult as this may be for some to understand, these are the principles which govern proceedings before this Tribunal at all times, even if application of these principles on occasion renders results which for some, are hard to swallow.

. . .

19. I wish to draw attention to the matter of *res judicata,* which was referred to by both the Appellant and the Prosecutor in their written briefs[21]. I wish to briefly discuss the applicability of this principle to the case in hand, noting that the Appeals Chamber has now reviewed its Decision.

20. The principle of *res judicata* is well settled in international law as being one of those "general principles of law recognized by civilised nations", referred to in Article 38 of the Statutes of the Permanent Court of International Justice ("PCIJ") and the International Court of Justice ("ICJ").[22] As such, it is a principle which should be applied by the Tribunal. The principle can be enunciated as meaning that, once a case has been decided by a final and valid judgement rendered by a competent tribunal, the same issue may not be disputed again between the same parties before a court of law[23].

---

[20] Jean-B..sco Barayagwiza v. The Prosecutor, *Decision*, Case no. ICTR-97-19-AR72, 3 November 1999 (the 'Decisio.. . § 111.

[21] *Brief .. Support of the Prosecutor's Motion for Review or Reconsideration of the Appeals Chamber Decisio.. ndered on 3 November 1999 in Jean-Bosco Barayagwiza v. The Prosecutor following the Orders of the Ap..eals Chamber Dated 25 November 1999,* § 74. *Appellant's Response to Prosecutor's Motion for Review .. Reconsideration of the Appeals Chamber Decision Rendered on 3 November 1999 in Jean-Bosco Barayagw..za v. The Prosecutor and Request for Stay of Execution,* § 17. *Prosecutor's Reply to the Appellant's Respons.. to the Prosecutor's Motion for Review or Reconsideration of the Appeals Chamber Decision Render.. .n 3 November 1999 in Jean-Bosco Barayagwiza v. The Prosecutor and Request for Stay of Executi..* § 21.

[22] *See* J..e Anzilotti's dissenting opinion in the *Chorzow Factory Case* (Interpretation), PCIJ Series A (1927), ..t 27. *See* also PCIJ, Advisory Committee of Jurists: *Procès-verbaux of the Proceedings of the Commi.. June 16-July 24, 1920, with Annexes*, The Hague, 1920, pp. 315-316.

[23] *Effec.. .wards of Compensation made by the United Nations Administrative Tribunal*, ICJ Reports 1954, p. 47.

21. ‌he rationale behind the principle is that security is required in juridical relations. The de ‌rminative and obligatory character of a judgement prevents the parties from contem ‌ating the possibility of not complying with the decision or alternatively from seeking ‌e same or another court to decide in a different manner. At the same time it is underst‌d that only final judgements are considered *res judicata*, as judgements of lower courts c ‌n generally take advantage of appellate proceedings.

22. ‌e impact of the Appeals Chamber Decision is twofold. On the one hand the Appea‌ ‌hamber decided to allow an appeal[24] against a decision of Trial Chamber II[25] which ‌smissed a preliminary objection by the accused based on lack of personal jurisdi‌ ‌n, on the grounds *inter alia*, that the fundamental human rights of the accused to a fair an‌ ‌xpeditious trial were violated as a result of his arrest and long detention in Camer‌ ‌ before being transferred to the U.N. Detention Facilities in Arusha. On the other hand, ‌e Decision "DISMISSE[D] THE INDICTMENT with prejudice to the Prosec‌ ‌r."[26] This rendered the Decision final and definitive, as stated by the Appeals Cham‌ in its decision today.[27]

23. ‌e International Court of Justice has held:

> It is contended that the question of the Applicants' legal right or interest was settled by ‌e [1962][28] Judgement and cannot now be reopened. As regards the issue of preclusion, ‌e Court finds it unnecessary to pronounce on various issues which have been raised in ‌is connection, such as whether a decision on a preliminary objection constitutes a *res* ‌*dicata* in the proper sense of that term, --whether it ranks as a "decision" for the ‌rposes of Article 59 of the Court's Statute, or as "final" within the meaning of Article ‌). The essential point is that a decision on a preliminary objection can never be ‌eclusive of a matter appertaining to its merits, whether or not it has in fact been dealt ‌th in connection with the preliminary objection".[29]

24. ‌domestic jurisdictions a preliminary objection on lack of competence, raised by a party be‌ ‌e a court does not prevent the matter being brought before the competent court. However ‌some decisions on preliminary points which are primarily within the competence

---

[24] *Supra* ‌e 20, § 113(1).
[25] Prose‌ v. Barayagwiza, *Decision on the Extremely Urgent Motion by the Defence for Orders to Review and/or* ‌*y the Arrest and Provisional Detention of the Suspect*, Case No. ICTR-97-19-I, 17 November 1998, a‌ ‌secutor v. Barayagwiza, *Corrigendum*, Case No. ICTR-97-19-I, 24 November 1998.
[26] *Supra* no‌ 20, § 113(2).
[27] § 49.
[28] *South W‌t Africa Cases (Ethiopia v. South Africa; Liberia v. South Africa) Preliminary Objections*, ICJ Reports. 1‌2, p. 319.
[29] *South* ‌*t Africa, Second phase, Judgement*, ICJ Reports. 1966, p. 6 at § 59.

of the co t acquire the force of *res judicata* on the question decided and the court is bound by its ow decisions.[30]

25. In this Tribunal, Article 25 of the Statute opens up the possibility for review of "final" decisions, if certain criteria are satisfied. The Appeals Chamber has clearly explaine this in its decision today. It is clear to me that if the Statute provides for a "final" decision be reviewed, when a Chamber acts pursuant to this provision, the principle of *res judic ta* does not apply.

26. S ne common law systems consider that dismissal of an indictment with prejudice bars the ght to bring an action again on the same issue and is, therefore, *res judicata*.[31] The insta case has not been litigated on the merits. What seems to be "final" is the issue of the prejudice to the Prosecutor, because the Prosecutor was barred from bringing the case before th Tribunal again. As I understood it, the Decision considered the finding of "prejudic to the Prosecutor" as a form of punishment due to the violations of fundamental human ri ts committed by the Prosecutor against the Appellant.[32]

27. I e new facts brought before the Appeals Chamber under Article 25 mean that the Prosecut is responsible for less extensive violations (as accepted by the Appeals Chamber today),[33] e cannot be punished because of them, the dismissal cannot be with prejudice to her and h ce the Decision must be amended. That is what we are deciding today.

28. nan rights treaties provide that when a state[34] violates fundamental human rights, it is obli d to ensure that appropriate domestic remedies are in place to put an end to such

[30] The di ction in the civil law systems between *peremptory* (which put an end to the procedure) and *dilatory* (w h simply delay the procedure) preliminary objections is very useful.
[31] This con pt is unknown to civil law systems.
[32] *Supr* 20, § 76.
[33] § 72.
[34] In these aties, the "subject-parties" are always States. *See* Article 2.1 ICCPR; Article 1 ECHR; Article 1.1 ACHR. T nter-American Court of Human Rights held that "as far as concerns the human rights protected by the C ntion, the jurisdiction of the organs established thereunder refer exclusively to the international respons of States and not to that of individuals" (*International Responsibility for the Promulgation and Enforce of Laws in Violation of the Convention (Articles 1 and 2 of the American Convention on Human Rights*). ory Opinion OC-14/94 of December 9, 1994, Series A No. 14, § 56.

violation and in certain circumstances to provide for fair compensation to the injured party.[35]

29. hough the Tribunal is not a State, it is following such a precedent to compensate the Ap nt for the violation of his human rights. As it is impossible to turn back the clock. nk that the remedy decided by the Appeals Chamber fulfills the international requirements.

. . .

30. ally, I wish to emphasise that the Appeals Chamber made its Decision, based on certain s which were presented before it at that time. The new facts which are before the Appe hamber now, change its position. If these facts which the Appeals Chamber has conclud to be new facts and which are discussed in today's decision, had been before the Appeals hamber when considering the Decision, it is my opinion that the Appeals Chamb ould have reached a different decision at that time.

Done in th English and French, the English text being authoritative.

s/.
Rafael Nieto-Navia

Dated 1st day of March 2000
At The H gue,
The Neth lands.

---

[35] Article ECHR; Article 63.1, ACHR. International jurisprudence has considered a "general concept of law" that ations of international obligations which cause harm deserve adequate reparation (*Factory at Chorzów,* *isdiction*, Judgement No. 8, 1927, P.C.I.J., Series A, No. 9, p.21; *Factory at Chorzów, Merits*, Judgement . 13, 1928, P.C.I.J., Series A, No. 17, p. 29.

SEPARATE OPINION OF JUDGE SHAHABUDDEEN

1. This is an important case; it is not every day that a court overturns its previous decision to liberate an indicted person. This is what happens now. New facts justify and require that result. But possible implications for the working of the infant criminal justice system of the international community need to be borne in mind. Because of this, and also because I agreed with the previous decision, I believe that I should explain why I support the present decision to cancel out the principal effect of the former.

(i) The limits of the present hearing

2. Except on one point, I was not able to agree with the grounds on which the previous decision rested. However, the points on which I differed are not now open for discussion. This is because the present motion of the Prosecutor has to be dealt with by way of review and not by way of reconsideration. Under review, the motion has to be approached on the footing that the earlier findings of the Appeals Chamber stand, save to the extent to which it can be seen that those findings would themselves have been different had certain new facts been available to the Appeals Chamber when the original decision was made; under that procedure, it is not therefore possible to challenge the previous holdings of the Appeals Chamber as incorrect on the basis on which they were made. By contrast, under reconsideration, the appeal would have been reopened, with the result that that kind of challenge would have been possible, as I apprehend is desired by the prosecution. To cover all the requests made by the prosecution, it is thus necessary to say a word on its motion for reconsideration. I agree that the motion should not be granted. These are my reasons:

3. Decisions rendered within the International Criminal Tribunal for the former Yugoslavia ("ICTY") on the competence of a Chamber to reconsider a decided point vary from the exercise of a relatively free power of reconsideration to a denial of any such power based on the statement, made in *Kordić*, "that motions to reconsider are not provided for in the Rules and do not form part of the procedures of the International

Tribunal".[1] Where the decisions suggest a relatively free power of reconsideration, they concern something in the nature of an operationally passing position taken in the course of continuing proceedings; in such situations the Chamber remains seised of the matter and competent, not acting capriciously but observing due caution, to revise its position on the way to rendering the ultimate decision. In situations of more lasting consequence, it appears to me that the absence of rules does not conclude the issue as to how a judicial body should behave where complaint is made that its previous decision was fundamentally flawed, and more particularly where that body is a court of last resort, as is the Appeals Chamber. Not surprisingly, in ^*elebići* the Appeals Chamber of the ICTY introduced a qualification in stating that "in the absence of particular circumstances justifying a Trial Chamber or the Appeals Chamber to reconsider one of its decisions, motions for reconsideration do not form part of the procedure of the International Tribunal".[2] The first branch of that statement is important, including its non-reproduction of the *Kordić* words "that motions to reconsider are not provided for in the Rules": the implication of the omission seems to be that the fact that the Rules do not so provide is not by itself determinative of the issue whether or not the power of reconsideration exists in "particular circumstances". Alternatively, the omitted words were not intended to deny the inherent jurisdiction of a judicial body to reconsider its decision in "particular circumstances".

4. Circumscribed as they evidently are, it is hard, and perhaps not in the interest of the policy of the law, to attempt exhaustively to define "particular circumstances" which might justify reconsideration. It is clear, however, that such circumstances include a case in which the decision, though apparently *res judicata*, is void, and therefore non-existent

---

[1] *Kordić*, IT-95-14/2-PT, 15 February 1999. And see similarly *Kovačević*, IT-97-24-PT, 30 June 1998.
[2] Order of the Appeals Chamber on Hazim Delić's Emergency Motion to Reconsider Denial of Request for Provisional Release, IT-96-21-A, 1 June 1999.

in law, for the reason that a procedural irregularity has caused a failure of natural justice.[3] An aspect of that position was put this way by the presiding member of the Appellate Committee of the British House of Lords:

> In principle it must be that your Lordships, as the ultimate court of appeal, have power to correct any injustice caused by an earlier order of this House. There is no relevant statutory limitation on the jurisdiction of the House in this regard and therefore its inherent jurisdiction remains unfettered. In *Cassell & Co Ltd v. Broome (No.2)* [1972] 2 All ER 849, [1972] AC 1136 your Lordships varied an order for costs already made by the House in circumstances where the parties had not had a fair opportunity to address argument on the point.
>
> However, it should be made clear that the House will not reopen any appeal save in circumstances where, through no fault of a party, he or she has been subjected to an unfair procedure. Where an order has been made by the House in a particular case there can be no question of that decision being varied or rescinded by a later order made in the same case just because it is thought that the first order is wrong.[4]

5. I understand this to mean that, certainly in the case of a court of last resort, there is inherent jurisdiction to reopen an appeal if a party had been "subjected to an unfair procedure". I see no reason why the principle involved does not apply to criminal matters if a useful purpose can be served, particularly where, as here, the decision in question has not been acted upon.

6. I have referred to unfairness in procedure because it appears to me that this is the criterion which is attracted by the posture of the Prosecutor's case. Was there such unfairness?

7. Whether a party was or was not "subjected to an unfair procedure" is a matter of substance, not technicality. If the party did not understand that an issue would be considered (which is the Prosecutor's contention), that could found a claim that it was disadvantaged. But, provided that that was understood and that there was opportunity to

---

[3] See, in English law, *Halsbury's Laws of England*, 4th edn., vol. 26, pp 279-280, para. 556, where mention is made of other situations in which a decision may be set aside and the proceedings reopened.

respond, I do not see that the procedure was unfair merely because a Chamber considered an issue not raised by the parties. The interests involved are not merely those of the parties; certainly, they are not interests submitted by them to adjudication on a consensual jurisdictional basis; they include the interests of the international community and are intended to be considered by a court exercising compulsory jurisdiction. In *Erdemović*[5] the Appeals Chamber raised, considered and decided issues not presented by the parties, observing that there was "nothing in the Statute or the Rules, nor in practices of international institutions or national judicial systems, which would confine its consideration of the appeal to the issues raised formally by the parties".[6]

8. Further, a Chamber need not echo arguments addressed to it; its reasoning may be its own.[7] When the present matter is examined, all that appears is that the Appeals Chamber in some cases used arguments other than those presented to it. The basic issue was one on which the parties had an opportunity to present their positions, namely, whether the rights of the appellant had been violated by undue delay so as to lead to lack of jurisdiction. For the reasons given below, I am satisfied that there is not any substance in the contention of the prosecution that it had no notice that certain questions would be determined. It is more to the point to say that the prosecution did not avail itself of opportunities to present its position on certain matters; in particular, it did not assist either the Trial Chamber or the Appeals Chamber with relevant material at the time when that assistance should have been given.

---

[4] *R v Bow Street Metropolitan Stipendiary Magistrate and others, ex parte Pinochet Ugarte (No 2)*, [1999] 1 All ER 577, HL, at pp. 585-586, per Lord Browne-Wilkinson.
[5] IT-96-22-A, 7 October 1997, para. 16.
[6] With respect, this can benefit from qualification in the case of the International Court of Justice. That court would be acting *ultra petita* if it decided issues (as distinguished from arguments concerning an issue) not presented by the parties, since the jurisdiction is consensual. See Sir Gerald Fitzmaurice, *The Law and Procedure of the International Court of Justice*, Vol. II (Cambridge, 1986), p. 531.

9. In short, there was no unfairness in procedure in this case. Accordingly, the previous decision of the Appeals Chamber cannot be set aside and the appeal reopened. It is thus not possible to accede to the Prosecutor's proposition, among others, that that decision was wrong when made and should for that reason be now changed.[8]

10. For the reasons given in today's judgment, the procedure of review is nevertheless available.[9] As mentioned above, the possibility of revision which this opens up is however limited to consideration of the question whether the same decision would have been rendered if certain new facts had been at the disposal of the Appeals Chamber, and, if not, what is the decision which would then have been given.

(ii) The Prosecutor's complaint that she had no notice of the intention of the Appeals Chamber to deal with the question of the legality of the detention between transfer and initial appearance

11. Before moving on, I shall pause over the question, alluded to above, as to whether the prosecution availed itself of opportunities to present its position on certain points. The question may be considered illustratively in relation to the issue of detention between the appellant's transfer from Cameroon to the Tribunal's detention unit in Arusha and his initial appearance before a Trial Chamber, extending from 19 November 1997 to 23 February 1998. The prosecution takes the position, which it stresses, that it had no opportunity to address this issue because it did not know that the Appeals Chamber would be dealing with it. That, if correct, is a sufficiently weighty matter to justify

---

[7] See the *"Lotus", (1927), PCIJ, Series A, No. 10*, p. 31; *Fisheries, ICJ Reports 1951*, p. 116, at p. 126; *Fisheries Jurisdiction (United Kingdom v. Iceland), Merits, ICJ Reports 1974*, p. 3, at pp. 9-10, para. 17. As to a distinction between issues and arguments, see Fitzmaurice, *supra*.
[8] Transcript, Appeals Chamber, 22 February 2000, p. 13.
[9] See also *Zejnil Delalić*, IT-96-21-T, 22 June 1998, paras. 38-40, which would seem, however, to apply the idea of review to an ordinary interlocutory decision even if it does not put an end to the case.

reconsideration, as it would show that the prosecution was subjected to an unfair procedure in the Appeals Chamber. So it should be examined.

12. The prosecution submitted that the issue of delay between transfer and initial appearance was not argued by the appellant in the course of the oral proceedings in the Trial Chamber and was not included in his grounds of appeal. Although, as will be seen, the appellant did include a claim on the point in his motion, I had earlier made a similar observation, noting that, in the Trial Chamber, "no issue was presented as to delay between transfer and initial appearance",[10] that the "Trial Chamber was not given any reason to believe that there was such an issue", and, in respect of the appeal proceedings, that it "does not appear that the Prosecutor thought that she was being called upon to meet an argument about delay between transfer and initial appearance".[11] But it seems to me that, apart from the action of the appellant, account has to be taken of the action of the Appeals Chamber and that the position changed with the issuing by the latter of its scheduling order of 3 June 1999; that order, referred to below, clearly raised the matter. After the order was made, the appellant went back to the claim which he had originally raised; equally, the prosecution gave its reaction. Thus, in the event, the Appeals Chamber did not pass on the matter without affording an opportunity to the Prosecutor to address the point.

13. To fill out this brief picture, it is right to consider the factual basis of the proposition that the appellant did include a claim on the point in his motion. As I noted

[10] Possibly, there was a misunderstanding as to the need for specific argument in the Trial Chamber, for the Presiding Judge said, as he properly could, "We have read the motion and the documents that have been attached to it so we have a general idea of what it is, so, counsel, if you may introduce your motion to highlight what you consider to be important issues that should get the Trial Chamber's attention". (See transcript, Trial Chamber, 11 September 1998, p. 4, Presiding Judge Sekule). Thus defence counsel was not expected to deal with each and every aspect of his written motion. He contended himself with speaking merely of "continued provisional detention" (ibid., pp. 12 and 14), and with referring to the "summary on the detention times" as set out in annexure DM2 to his motion and as explained below (ibid., p. 39).

[11] Separate opinion, 3 November 1999, p. 3, cited in part in the Brief in Support of the Prosecutor's Motion for Review, 1 December 1999, p. 8, para. 51.

at page 1 of a separate opinion appended to the decision of the Appeals Chamber of 3 November 1999, in paragraphs 2 and 9 of the motion the appellant complained of "continued provisional detention". Viewing the time when that complaint was made (three months after the transfer), he was thus also complaining of the detention following on his transfer, inclusive of delay between transfer and initial appearance. In fact, as I also pointed out, annexure DM2 to his motion spoke of "**98 days** of detention after transfer and before initial appearance" (original emphasis, but actually 96 days). Further, in paragraph 11 of his brief in support of that motion he referred to Articles 7, 8, 9 and 10 of the Universal Declaration of Human Rights, relating *inter alia* to protection of the law and to freedom from arbitrary arrest and detention. More particularly, he also referred to Article 9 of the International Covenant on Civil and Political Rights ("ICCPR"), stating that this required that "the accused should be brought before the court without delay". That was obviously a reference to paragraph 3 of Article 9 of the ICCPR which stipulates that "[a]nyone arrested or detained on a criminal charge shall be brought promptly before a judge or other officer authorized by law to exercise judicial power and shall be entitled to trial within a reasonable time or to release". It follows that, in his motion, the appellant did make a complaint on the matter to the Trial Chamber.

14. Now, how did the prosecution react to the appellant's complaint? The complaint having been made in the motion, and the motion being heard seven months after it was brought, it seems to me that, by the time when the motion was heard, the prosecution should have been in possession of all material relevant to the issue whether there was undue delay between transfer and initial appearance; it also had an opportunity at that stage to present all of that material together with supporting arguments. The record shows that it did not do so.

15. In the Trial Chamber, the prosecution did not file a response to the appellant's motion in which the appellant complained of delay between transfer and initial appearance. Indeed, some part of the oral hearing before the Trial Chamber on 11 September 1998 was taken up with this very fact - that the prosecution had not submitted a reply, with the consequential difficulty, about which the appellant

remonstrated, that he did not know exactly what issues the prosecution intended to challenge at the hearing before the Trial Chamber. In the words then used by his counsel, "... in an adversarial system we should not leave leeway for ambush".[12] In his reply, counsel for the prosecution simply said, "We didn't do it in this case and I have no explanation for that. ... we don't have an explanation for why we haven't followed our *usual practice*".[13] In turn, the Presiding Judge, though not sanctioning the prosecution, noted that what was done was contrary to the established procedure.[14] At the oral hearing before the Appeals Chamber on 22 February 2000, counsel for the prosecution took the position that there was no rule requiring the prosecution to file a response.[15] Counsel for the prosecution before the Trial Chamber had earlier made the same point.[16] They were both right. But that circumstance was not determinative. As the Presiding Judge of the Trial Chamber had made clear, it was the practice to file a response; and, as counsel for the prosecution later conceded at the oral hearing before the Appeals Chamber on 22 February 2000, the Presiding Judge "did draw the conclusion that [what was done] was contrary ... to the practice of the Tribunal".[17] Indeed, at the hearing before the Trial Chamber on 11 September 1998, counsel for the prosecution accepted, as has been seen, that the failure of the prosecution to submit a written reply was contrary to the "usual practice" of the prosecution itself.

16. The failure of the prosecution to respond to the appellant's complaint of undue delay between transfer and initial appearance did not of course remove the complaint. The dismissal of the appellant's motion included dismissal of that complaint. The complaint and its dismissal formed part of the record before the Appeals Chamber. This being so, it appears to me that at this stage the question of substance is whether the

---

[12] Transcript, Trial Chamber, 11 September 1998, p. 5.
[13] Ibid., p. 8, emphasis added.
[14] Ibid., p. 9.
[15] Transcript, Appeals Chamber, 22 February 2000, p. 105.
[16] Transcript, Trial Chamber, 11 September 1998, p. 8.

Prosecutor knew that the Appeals Chamber intended to deal with the complaint, and, if so, whether the Prosecutor had an opportunity to address it. The answer to both questions is in the affirmative. This results from the Appeals Chamber's scheduling order of 3 June 1999, referred to above.

17. That order required the parties "to address the following questions and provide the Appeals Chamber with all relevant documentation: ....4). The reason for any delay between the transfer of the Appellant to the Tribunal and his initial appearance". The requisition was made on the stated basis that the Appeals Chamber needed "additional information to decide the appeal". At the oral hearing in the Appeals Chamber on 22 February 2000, a question from the bench to counsel for the Prosecutor was this: "Did the prosecution understand from that, that the Appeals Chamber was proposing to consider reasons for any delay between transfer of the Appellant and his initial appearance?".[18] Counsel for the Prosecutor correctly answered in the affirmative. He also agreed that the prosecution did not object to the competence of the Appeals Chamber to consider the matter and did not ask for more time to respond to the request by the Appeals Chamber for additional information.[19] In fact, in paragraphs 17-20 of its response of 21 June 1999, the prosecution sought to explain the delay in so far as it then said that it could, stating that it had no influence over the scheduling of the initial appearance of accused persons, that these matters lay with the Trial Chambers and the Registrar, that assignment of defence counsel was made only on 5 December 1997, and that there was a judicial holiday from 15 December 1997 to 15 January 1998. In stating these things (how adequate they were being a different matter), the prosecution fell to be understood as having accepted that the Appeals Chamber would be dealing one way or another with the question to which those things were a response.

---

[17] Transcript, Appeals Chamber, 22 February 2000, p. 107.

18. Focusing on the issues as she saw them, the Prosecutor, as I understood her, submitted that the Appeals Chamber was confined to the issues presented by the parties. As indicated above, that is not entirely correct. The cases show that the leading principle is that the overriding task of the Tribunal is to discover the truth. Since this has to be done judicially, limits obviously exist as to permissible methods of search; and those limits have to be respected, for the Appeals Chamber is not an overseer. It cannot gratuitously intervene whenever it feels that something wrong was done: beyond the proper appellate boundaries, the decisions of the Trial Chamber are unquestionable. However, as is shown by *Erdemović*,[20] the Appeals Chamber can raise issues whether or not presented by a party, provided, I consider, that they lie within the prescribed grounds of appeal, that they arise from the record, and that the parties are afforded an opportunity to respond. I think that this was the position in this case.

19. As has been demonstrated above, the record before the Appeals Chamber included both a claim by the appellant that there was impermissible delay between transfer and initial appearance[21] and dismissal by the Trial Chamber of the motion which included that claim. Where an issue lying within the prescribed grounds of appeal is raised on the record, the Appeals Chamber can properly require the parties to submit additional information on the point; there is not any basis for suggesting, as the Prosecutor has done, that in this case the Appeals Chamber went outside of the appropriate limits in search of evidence.

20. In conclusion, it appears to me that the substance of the matter is that the Prosecutor had notice of the intention of the Appeals Chamber to deal with the point, had

---

[18] Ibid., p. 108.
[19] Ibid.
[20] IT-96-22-A, 7 October 1997.
[21] By contrast, the appellant's motion did not, in my opinion, include a claim that there was impermissible delay in the hearing of his habeas corpus motion.

an opportunity to address the point both before the Trial Chamber and the Appeals Chamber, and did address the point in her written response to the Appeals Chamber. In particular, the Prosecutor knew that the Appeals Chamber would be passing on the point and did not object to the competence of the Appeals Chamber to do so. Her approach fell to be understood as acquiescence in such competence. I accordingly return to my previous position that it is not possible to set aside the previous decision and to reopen the appeal, and that the only way of revisiting the matter is through the more limited method of review on the basis of discovery of new facts.

(iii) The Prosecutor's argument that the Appeals Chamber did not apply the proper test for determining whether there was a breach of the appellant's rights

21. In dealing with this argument by the Prosecutor, it would be useful to distinguish between the breach of a right and the remedy for a breach. The former will be dealt with in this section; the latter in the next.

22. An opinion which I appended to the decision given on 2 July 1998 by the Appeals Chamber of the ICTY in *Prosecutor v. Kovačević* included an observation to the effect that, because of the preparatory problems involved, the jurisprudence recognises that there is "need for judicial flexibility" in applying to the prosecution of war crimes the principle that criminal proceedings should be completed within a reasonable time. The prosecution correctly submits that, in determining whether there has been a breach of that principle, a court must weigh competing interests. As it was said in one case, the court "must balance the fundamental right of the individual to a fair trial within a reasonable time against the public interest in the attainment of justice in the context of the prevailing system of legal administration and the prevailing economic, social and cultural conditions to be found in" the territory concerned.[22] To do this, the court "should assess such factors

[22] *Bell v. Director of Public Prosecutions* [1985] 1 AC 937, PC.

as the length of and reason for the delay, the defendant's assertion of his right, and prejudice to the defendant".[23] The reason for the delay could of course include the complexity of the case and the conduct of the prosecuting authorities as well as that of the court as a whole.

23. These criteria are correct; but I do not follow why it is thought that they were not applied by the Appeals Chamber. Their substance was considered in paragraphs 103-106 of the previous decision of the Appeals Chamber, footnote 268 whereof specifically referred to the leading cases of *Barker v. Wingo* and *R. v. Smith*, among others. Applying that jurisprudence in this case, it is difficult to see how the balance came out against the appellant. On the facts as they appeared to the Appeals Chamber, the delay was long; it was due to the Tribunal; no adequate reasons were given for it; the appellant repeatedly complained of it; and, there being nothing to rebut a reasonable presumption that it prejudiced his position, a fair inference could be drawn that it did.

24. The breach of the appellant's rights appears even more clearly when it is considered that the jurisprudence which produced principles about balancing competing interests developed largely, if not wholly, out of cases in which the accused was in fact brought before a judicial officer shortly after being charged, but in which, for one reason or another, the subsequent trial took a long time to approach completion. By contrast, the problem here is not that the proceedings had taken too long to complete, but that they had taken too long to begin. It is not suggested that those principles are irrelevant to the resolution of the present problem; what is suggested is that, in applying them to the present problem, the difference referred to has to be taken into account. To find a solution it is necessary to establish what is the proper judicial approach to detention in the early stages of a criminal case, and especially in the pre-arraignment phase.

---

[23] *Barker v. Wingo*, 407 US 514 (1972); and see *R. v. Smith* [1989] 2 Can. S.C.R. 1120, and *Morin v. R.* [1992] 1 S.C.R. 771.

25. The matter turns, it appears to me, on a distinction between the right of a person to a trial within a reasonable time and the right of a person to freedom from arbitrary interference with his liberty. The right to a trial within a reasonable time can be violated even if there has never been any arrest or detention; by contrast, a complaint of arbitrary interference with liberty can only be made where a person has been arrested or detained. I am not certain that the distinction was recognised by the prosecution.[24] In the view of its counsel, which he said was based on the decision of the Appeals Chamber and on other cases, the object of the Rule 62 requirement for the accused to be brought "without delay" before the Trial Chamber was to allow him "to know the formal charges against him" and to enable him "to mount a defence".[25] The submission was that, in this case, both of these purposes had been served before the initial appearance, the indictment having been given to the appellant while he was still in Cameroon. But it seems to me that, as counsel later accepted,[26] there was yet another purpose, and that that purpose could only be served if there was an initial appearance. That purpose – a fundamentally important one – was to secure to the detained person a right to be placed "without delay" within the protection of the judicial power and consequently to ensure that there was no arbitrary curtailment of his right to liberty. That purpose is a major one in the work of an institution of this kind; it is worthy of being marked.

26. For present purposes, the law seems straightforward. It is not in dispute that the controlling instruments of the Tribunal reflect the internationally recognised requirement that a detained person shall be brought "without delay" to the judiciary as required by Rule 40*bis*(J) and Rule 62 of the Tribunal's Rules of Procedure and Evidence, or "promptly" as it is said in Article 5(3) of the European Convention on Human Rights and Article 9(3) of the ICCPR, the latter being alluded to by the appellant in paragraph 11 of

---

[24] Transcript, Appeals Chamber, 22 February 2000, pp. 97-98.
[25] Ibid., pp. 72-73.
[26] Ibid., pp. 95-97.

the brief in support of his motion of 19 February 1998, as mentioned above. It will be convenient to refer to one of these provisions, namely, Article 5(3) of the European Convention on Human Rights. This provides that "[e]veryone arrested or detained in accordance with the provisions of paragraph 1.*c* of this article [relating to arrests for reasonable suspicion of having committed an offence] shall be brought promptly before a judge or other officer authorised by law to exercise judicial power ...".

27. So first, as to the purpose of these provisions. Apart from the general entitlement to a trial within a reasonable time, it is judicially recognised that the purpose is to guarantee to the arrested person a right to be brought promptly within the protection of the judiciary and to ensure that he is not arbitrarily deprived of his right to liberty.[27] The European Court of Human Rights, whose case law on the subject is persuasive, put the point by observing that the requirement of promptness "enshrines a fundamental human right, namely the protection of the individual against arbitrary interferences by the State with his right to liberty.... Judicial control of interferences by the executive with the individual's right to liberty is an essential feature of the guarantee embodied in Article 5§3 [of the European Convention on Human Rights], which is intended to minimise the risk of arbitrariness. Judicial control is implied by the rule of law, 'one of the fundamental principles of a democratic society ...'".[28]

28. Second, as to the tolerable period of delay, the decision of the Appeals Chamber of 3 November 1999 correctly recognised that this is short. The work of the United Nations Human Rights Committee shows that it is about four days. In *Portorreal v. Dominican Republic*, a period of 50 hours was held to be too short to constitute delay.[29]

---

[27] Eur. Court H.R., Schiesser judgment of 4 December 1979, Series A no. 34, p. 13, para. 30.
[28] Eur. Court H.R., Brogan and Others judgment of 29 November 1988, Series A no. 145-B, p. 32, para. 58.
[29] United Nations Human Rights Committee, Communication No. 188/1984 (5 November 1987).

But a period of 35 days was considered too much in *Kelly v. Jamaica.*[30] In *Jijón v. Ecuador*[31] a five-day delay was judged to be violative of the rule.

29. The same tendency in the direction of brevity is evident in the case law of the European Court of Human Rights. In *McGoff*[32], on his extradition from the Netherlands to Sweden, the applicant was kept in custody for 15 days before he was brought to the court. That was held to be in violation of the rule. *De Jong, Baljet and van den Brink*[33] concerned judicial proceedings in the army. "[E]ven taking due account of the exigencies of military life and military justice", the European Court of Human Rights considered that a delay of seven days was too long.

30. In *Koster,*[34] which also concerned judicial proceedings in the army, a five-day delay was held to be in breach of the rule. The fact that the period included a weekend and two-yearly military manoeuvres, in which members of the court - a military court - had been participating was disregarded; in the view of the European Court of Human Rights, the rights of the accused took precedence over matters which were "foreseeable".[35] The military manoeuvres "in no way prevented the military authorities from ensuring that the Military Court was able to sit soon enough to comply with the requirements of [Article 5(3) of the European Convention on Human Rights], *if necessary on Saturday or Sunday*".[36]

---

[30] United Nations Human Rights Committee, Communication No. 253/1987 (8 April 1991).
[31] United Nations Human Rights Committee, Communication No. 277/1988 (26 March 1992).
[32] Eur. Court H.R., McGoff judgment of 26 October 1984, Series A no. 83, pp. 26-27, para. 27.
[33] Eur. Court H.R., de Jong, Baljet and van den Brink judgment of 22 May 1984, Series A no. 77, p. 25, para. 52.
[34] Eur. Court H.R., Koster judgment of 28 November 1991, Series A no. 221.
[35] Ibid., para. 25.
[36] Ibid., emphasis added.

31. No doubt, as it was said in *de Jong, Baljet and van den Brink*, "The issue of promptness must always be assessed in each case according to its special features".[37] The same thing was said in *Brogan*.[38] But this does not markedly enlarge the normal period. *Brogan* was a case of terrorism; the European Court of Human Rights was not altogether unresponsive to the implications of that fact, to which the state concerned indeed appealed.[39] Yet the Court took the view that a period of six days and sixteen and a half hours was too long; indeed, it considered that even a shorter period of four days and six hours was outside the constraints of the relevant provision. The Court began its reasoning by saying:

> No violation of Article 5§3 [of the European Convention on Human Rights] can arise if the arrested person is released 'promptly' before any judicial control of his detention would have been feasible ... If the arrested person is not released promptly, he is entitled to a prompt appearance before a judge or judicial officer.[40]

32. Thus, in measuring permissible delay, the Court started out by having regard to the time within which it would have been "feasible" to establish judicial control of the detention in the circumstances of the case. The idea of feasibility obviously introduced a margin of flexibility in the otherwise strict requirement of promptness. But how to fix the limits of this flexibility? The Court looked at the "object and purpose of Article 5", or, as it said, at the "aim and ... object" of the Convention", and stated that –

> the degree of flexibility attaching to the notion of 'promptness' is limited, even if the attendant circumstances can never be ignored for the purposes of the assessment under paragraph 3. Whereas promptness is to be assessed in each case according to its special features ..., the significance to be attached to those features can never be taken to the point of impairing the very essence of the right guaranteed by Article 5§3 [of the European Convention on Human Rights], that is to the point of effectively

---

[37] Eur. Court H.R., de Jong, Baljet and van den Brink judgment of 22 May 1984, Series A no. 77, p. 25, para. 52.
[38] Eur. Court H.R., Brogan and Others judgment of 29 November 1988, Series A no. 145-B, para. 59.
[39] Ibid., para. 62.
[40] Ibid., para. 58.

> negativing the State's obligation to ensure a prompt release or a prompt appearance before a judicial authority.[41]

33. In paragraph 62 of its judgment in *Brogan*, the European Court of Human Rights again mentioned that the "scope for flexibility in interpreting and applying the notion of 'promptness' is very limited". Thus, although the Court appreciated the special circumstances which terrorism represented, it said that "[t]he undoubted fact that the arrest and detention of the applicants were inspired by the legitimate aim of protecting the community as a whole from terrorism is not on its own sufficient to ensure compliance with the specific requirements of Article 5§3".[42]

34. To refer again to *McGoff*, in that case the European Commission of Human Rights recalled that, in an earlier matter, it had expressed the view that a period of four days was acceptable; "it also accepted five days, but that was in exceptional circumstances".[43]

35. In the case at bar, counting from the time of transfer to the Tribunal's detention unit in Arusha (19 November 1997) to the date of initial appearance before a Trial Chamber (23 February 1998), the period - the Arusha period - was 96 days, or *nearly 20 times the maximum acceptable period of delay.*

36. As a matter of juristic logic, any flexibility in applying the requirements concerning time to the case of war crimes has to find its justification not in the nature of the crimes themselves, but in the difficulties of investigating, preparing and presenting cases relating to them. Consequently, that flexibility is not licence for disregarding the requirements where they can be complied with. It is only "the austerity of tabulated legalism", an idea not much favoured where, as here, a generous interpretation is called

---

[41] Ibid., para. 59.
[42] Ibid., para. 62.
[43] Eur. Court H.R., McGoff judgment of 26 October 1984, Series A no. 83, Annex, Opinion of the Commission, p. 31, para. 28.

for[44], which could lead to the view that, once a crime is categorised as a war crime, that suffices to justify the conclusion that the requirements concerning time may be safely put aside.

37. In this case, it is not easy to see what difficulty beset the authorities in bringing the appellant from the Tribunal's detention unit to the Trial Chamber. That scarcely inter-galactic passage involved no more than a fifteen minute drive by motor car on a macadamised road. To plead the character of the crimes in justification of the manifest breach of an applicable requirement which was both of overriding importance and capable of being respected with the same ease as in the ordinary case is to transform an important legal principle into a statement of affectionate aspiration.

38. On the facts as they earlier appeared to it, the Appeals Chamber could not come to any conclusion other than that the rights of the appellant in respect of the period between transfer and initial appearance had been breached, and very badly so. As today's decision finds, the new facts do not show that they were not breached. I agree, however, that the new facts show that the breach was not as serious as it at first appeared, it being now clear that defence counsel, although having opportunities, did not object and could be treated as having acquiesced in the passage of time during most of the relevant period.

(iv) Whether a breach could be remedied otherwise than by release

39. Now for the question of remedy, assuming the existence of a breach. In this respect, the prosecution argues that, if there was a breach of the appellant's rights, it was open to the Appeals Chamber to grant some form of compensatory relief short of release and that it should have done so. In support, notice may be taken of a view that, particularly though not exclusively in the case of war crimes, the remedy for a breach of

---

[44] See the criticism made by Lord Wilberforce in *Minister of Home Affairs v. Fisher* [1980] AC 319, PC, at 328 G-H.

the principle that a trial is to be held within a reasonable time may take the form of payment of monetary compensation or of adjustment of any sentence ultimately imposed, custody being meanwhile continued.[45]

40. That view is useful, although not altogether free from difficulty;[46] it is certainly not an open-ended one. If the concern of the law with the liberty of the person, as demonstrated by the above-mentioned attitude of the courts, means anything, it is necessary to contemplate a point of time at which the accused indisputably becomes entitled to release and dismissal of the indictment. In this respect, it is to be observed that, according to the European Commission of Human Rights, contrary to an opinion of the German Federal Court, in 1983 a committee of three judges of the German Constitutional Court held that "unreasonable delays of criminal proceedings might under certain circumstances only be remedied by discontinuing such proceedings".[47] As is shown by the last paragraph of the report of *Bell's* case, *supra*, the only reason why a formal order prohibiting further proceedings was not made in that case by the Privy Council was because it was understood that the practice in Jamaica was that there would be no further proceedings. Paragraph 108 of the decision of the Appeals Chamber of 3 November 1999 cites cases from other territories in which further proceedings were in fact prohibited. I find no fault with the position taken in those cases; true, those cases concerned delay in holding and completing the trial, but I do not accept that the principle on which they rest is necessarily inapplicable to extended pre-arraignment delay.

41. More importantly, the view that relief short of release is possible is subject to any statutory obligation to effect a release. In this respect, in its previous decision the

---

[45] See, inter alia, P. van Dijk and G.J.H. van Hoof, *Theory and Practice of the European Convention on Human Rights*, 3rd ed. (The Hague, 1998), pp. 449-450; and see generally the cases cited therein, including *Neubeck*, D & R 41 (1985), p. 57, para. 131; *H v. Federal Republic of Germany*, D & R 41 (1985), pp. 253-254; and *Eckle*, Eur. Court H.R., Eckle judgment of 15 July 1982, Series A no.51, p. 31, para. 67.
[46] See discussion in van Dijk and van Hoop, *loc.cit.*

Appeals Chamber held that Rule 40*bis* of the Tribunal's Rules of Procedure and Evidence applied to the Cameroon period of detention. I respectfully disagreed with that view and still do, but it is the decision of the Appeals Chamber which matters; and so I proceed on the basis that the Rule applied. Now, Sub-Rule (H) of that Rule provided as follows:

> The total period of provisional detention shall in no case exceed 90 days, at the end of which, in the event that the indictment has not been confirmed and an arrest warrant signed, the suspect *shall be released* ... (emphasis added).

42. Consistently with the judicial approach to detention in the early phases of a criminal case, the object of the cited provision is to control arbitrary interference with the liberty of the person by guaranteeing him a right to be released if he is not charged within the stated time. In keeping with that object, the Rule, which has the force of law, provides its own sanction. Where that sanction comes into operation through breach of the 90-day limit set by the Rule, release is both automatic and compulsory: a court order may be made but is not necessary. The detained person has to be mandatorily released in obedience to the command of the Rule: no consideration can be given to the possibility of keeping him in custody and granting him a remedy in the form of a reduction of sentence (if any) or of payment of compensation; any discretion as to alternative forms of remedy is excluded, however serious were the allegations.

43. In effect, the premise of the conclusion reached by the Appeals Chamber that the appellant had to be released was the Chamber's interpretation, on the facts then before it, that the Rule applied to the Cameroon period of detention. These being review proceedings and not appeal proceedings, the premise would continue to apply, and so would the conclusion, unless displaced by new facts.

---

[47] *H v. Federal Republic of Germany*, application no. 10884/84, D & R, no. 41, decision of 13 December 1984, p. 253.

(v) Whether there are new facts

44. So now for the question whether there are new facts. The temptation to use national decisions in this area may be rightly restrained by the usual warnings of the dangers involved in facile transposition of municipal law concepts to the plane of international law. Such borrowings were more frequent in the early or formative stages of the general subject; now that autonomy has been achieved, there is less reason for such recourse. It is possible to argue that the current state of criminal doctrine in international law approximates to that of the larger subject at an earlier phase and that accordingly a measure of liberality in using domestic law ideas is both natural and permissible in the field of criminal law. But it is not necessary to pursue the argument further. The reason is that, altogether apart from the question whether a particular line of municipal decisions is part of the law of the Tribunal, no statutory authority needs to be cited to enable a court to benefit from the scientific value of the thinking of other jurists, provided that the court remains master of its own house. Thus, nothing prevents a judge from consulting the reasoning of judges in other jurisdictions in order to work out his own solution to an issue before him; the navigation lights offered by the reflections of the former can be welcome without being obtrusive. This is how I propose to proceed.

45. The books are full of statements, and rightly so, concerning the caution which has to be observed, as a general matter, in admitting fresh evidence. Latham CJ noted that "[t]hese are general principles which should be applied to both civil and criminal trials".[48] Accordingly, there is to be borne in mind the principle familiar in civil cases, somewhat quaintly expressed in one of them, that it is the "duty of [a party] to bring forward his

[48] *Green v. R.* (1939) 61 C.L.R. 167, at 175.

whole case at once, and not to bring it forward piecemeal as he found out the objections in his way".[49]

46. The prosecution advanced a claim to several new facts. Agreeably to the caution referred to, the Appeals Chamber has not placed reliance on all of them. I shall deal with two which were accepted, beginning with the statement of Ambassador Scheffer as to United States intervention with the government of Cameroon. Five questions arise in respect of that statement.

47. The first question is whether the Ambassador's statement concerns a "new fact" within the meaning of Article 25 of the Statute. It has to be recognised that there can be difficulty in drawing a clear line of separation between a new fact within the meaning of that Article of the Statute and additional evidence within the meaning of Rule 115 of the Tribunal's Rules of Procedure and Evidence. A new fact is generically in the nature of additional evidence. The differentiating specificity is this: additional evidence, though not being merely cumulative, goes to the proof of facts which were in issue at the hearing; by contrast, evidence of a new fact is evidence of a distinctly new feature which was not in issue at the trial. In this case, there has not been an issue of fact in the previous proceedings as to whether the government of the United States had intervened. True, the intervention happened before the hearing, but that does not make the fact of the intervention any the less new. As is implicitly recognised by the wording of Article 25 of the Statute and Rule 120 of the Rules of Procedure and Evidence of the Tribunal, the circumstance that a fact was in existence at the time of trial does not automatically disqualify it from being regarded as new; the newness has to be in relation to the facts previously before the court. In my opinion, Ambassador Scheffer's statement is evidence of a new fact.

---

[49] *In re New York Exchange, Limited* (1888) 39 Ch. D. 415, at 420, CA.

48. The second question is whether the new fact "could not have been discovered [at the time of the proceedings before the original Chamber] through the exercise of due diligence" within the meaning of Rule 120 of the Rules. The position of the prosecution is that it did ask Ambassador Scheffer to intervene with the government of Cameroon. This being so, it is reasonable to hold that the prosecution knew that the requested intervention was needed to end a delay caused by Cameroon, and that it was also in a position to know that the intervention had in fact taken place and that it involved the activities in question. It is therefore difficult to find that the material in question could not have been discovered with due diligence. In this respect, I agree with the appellant.

49. But, for the reasons given in today's judgment, that does not end the matter. Certainly the general rule is that " the interests of justice" will not suffice to authorise the admission of material which was available at trial, diligence being a factor in determining availability. The principle of finality supports that view. But, as has been recognised by the Appeals Chamber of the ICTY, "the principle [of finality] would not operate to prevent the admission of evidence that would assist in determining whether there could have been a miscarriage of justice".[50] As was also observed by that Chamber,[51] "the principle of finality must be balanced against the need to avoid a miscarriage of justice". I see no reason why the necessity to make that balance does not apply to a review.

50. Thus, there has to be recognition of the possibility of there being a case in which, notwithstanding the absence of diligence, the material in question is so decisive in demonstrating mistake that the court in its discretion is obliged to admit it in the upper interests of justice. This was done in one case in which an appeal court observed, "All the evidence tendered to us could have been adduced at the trial: indeed, three of the witnesses, whom we have heard... did give evidence at the trial. Nevertheless we have

---

[50] *Tadić*, IT-94-1-A, 15 October 1998, para. 72. The context suggests that the word "not" in the expression "not available" in line 8 of para. 35 of that decision was inserted *per incuriam*.
[51] Ibid., para. 35.

thought it necessary, exercising our discretion in the interests of justice, to receive" their evidence.[52] It is not the detailed underlying legislation which is important, but the principle to be discerned.

51. The principle was more recently affirmed by the Supreme Court of Canada in the case of *R v. Warsing*.[53] There the leading opinion recalled an earlier view that "the criterion of due diligence... is not applied strictly in criminal cases" and said: "It is desirable that due diligence remain only one factor and its absence, particularly in criminal cases, should be assessed in light of other circumstances. If the evidence is compelling and the interests of justice require that it be admitted then the failure to meet the test should yield to permit its admission".[54] In the same opinion, it was later affirmed that "a failure to meet the due diligence requirement should not 'override accomplishing a just result'".[55]

52. It may be thought that an analogous principle can be collected from *Aleksovski*, in which the Appeals Chamber of the ICTY held "that, in general, accused before this Tribunal have to raise all possible defences, where necessary in the alternative, during trial ..." ,[56] but stated that it "will nevertheless consider" a new defence. Clearly, if the new defence was sound in law and convincing in fact, it would have been entertained in the higher interests of justice notwithstanding the general rule.

53. Thus, having regard to the superior demands of justice, I would read the reference in Rule 120 to a new fact which "could not have been discovered through the exercise of due diligence" as directory, and not mandatory or peremptory. In this respect, it is said that the "language of a statute, however mandatory in form, may be deemed directory

---

[52] See *R v. Lattimore* (1976) 62 Cr. App. R. 53, at 56.
[53] [1998] 3 S.C.R. 579.
[54] Ibid., para. 51 of the opinion of Justices Cory, Iacobucci, Major and Binnie.
[55] Ibid., para. 56.
[56] See paragraph 51 of IT-95-14/1-A of 24 March 2000.

whenever legislative purpose can best be carried out by [adopting a directory] construction".[57] Here, the overriding purpose of the provision is to achieve justice. Justice is denied by adopting a mandatory interpretation of the text; a directory approach achieves it. This approach, it is believed, is consonant with the broad view that, as it has been said, "the relation of rules of practice to the work of justice is intended to be that of handmaid rather than mistress, and the Court ought not to be so far bound and tied by rules, which are after all only intended as general rules of procedure, as to be compelled to do what will cause injustice in the particular case".[58] That remark was made about rules of civil procedure, but, with proper caution, the idea inspiring it applies generally to all rules of procedure to temper any tendency to rely too confidently, or too simplistically, on the maxim *dura lex, sed lex.*[59] I do not consider that this approach necessarily collides with the general principle regulating the interpretation of penal provisions and believe that it represents the view broadly taken in all jurisdictions.

54. The question then is whether, even if there was an absence of diligence, the material in this case so compellingly demonstrates mistake as to justify its admission. Ambassador Scheffer's statement makes it clear that the delay in Cameroon was due to the workings of the decision-making process in that country, that that process was expedited only after and as a result of his and his government's intervention with the highest authorities in Cameroon, that Cameroon was otherwise not ready to effect a transfer, and that accordingly the Tribunal was not to blame for any delay, as the Appeals Chamber thought it was. Has the Appeals Chamber to close its eyes to Ambassador Scheffer's statement, showing, as it does, the existence of palpable mistake bearing on the correctness of the previous conclusion? I think not.

---

[57] 82 *Corpus Juris Secundum* (Brooklyn, 1990), pp. 871-872, stating also, at p. 869, that "a statute may be mandatory in some respects, and directory in others". And see *Craies on Statute Law*, 7th edn. (London, 1971), pp. 62, 249-250, and 260-271.
[58] *In re Coles and Ravenshear* [1907] 1 K.B. 1, at 4.

55. The third question is which Chamber should process the significance of the new fact: Is it the Appeals Chamber? Or, is it the Trial Chamber? In the *Tadić* Rule 115 application, the ICTY Appeals Chamber took the position, in paragraph 30 of its Decision of 15 October 1998, that the "proper venue for a review application is the Chamber that rendered the final judgement". Well, this is a review and it is being conducted by the Chamber which gave the final judgement - namely, the Appeals Chamber. So the case falls within the *Tadić* proposition.

56. I would, however, add this: On the basis of the statement in question, there could be argument that the Appeals Chamber cannot itself assess a new fact where the Appeals Chamber is sitting on appeal. However, it appears to me that the statement need not be construed as intended to neutralise the implication of Rule 123 of the Rules of Procedure and Evidence of the Tribunal that the Appeals Chamber may itself determine the effect of a new fact in an appeal pending before it. That Rule states: "If the judgement to be reviewed is under appeal at the time the motion for review is filed, the Appeals Chamber may return the case to the Trial Chamber for disposition of the motion". The word "may" shows that the Appeals Chamber need not send the matter to the Trial Chamber but may deal with it itself. The admissibility of this course is supported by the known jurisprudence, which shows that matter in the nature of a new fact may be considered on appeal. Thus, in *R. v. Ditch* (1969) 53 Cr. App. R. 627, at p. 632, a post-trial confession by a co-accused was admitted on appeal as fresh or additional evidence, having been first heard *de bene esse* before being formally admitted.[60] Structures differ; it is the principle involved which matters. The jurisprudence referred to above in relation to mandatory and directory provisions also works to the same end. In my view, that end means this:

---

[59] Cited sometimes in legal discourse, as in *Serbian Loans*, P.C.I.J., Ser. A, No. 20-21, p. 56, dissenting opinion of Judge de Bustamante.

[60] Earlier cases suggested that this sort of evidence should be processed through the clemency machinery; but the position was changed by s. 23(2) of the Criminal Appeal Act 1968 (UK).

where the new fact is in its nature conclusive, it may be finally dealt with by the Appeals Chamber itself; a reference back to the Trial Chamber is required only where, without being conclusive, the new fact is of such strength that it might reasonably affect the verdict, whether the verdict would in fact be affected being left to the evaluation of the Trial Chamber.[61]

57. The fourth question is whether the new fact brought forward in Ambassador Scheffer's statement "could have been a decisive factor in reaching the decision", within the meaning of Article 25 of the Statute. The simple answer is "yes". As mentioned above, the decision of the Appeals Chamber proceeded on the basis that the Tribunal was responsible for the delay in Cameroon and that the latter was always ready to make a transfer. The Ambassador's statement shows that these things were not so.

58. The fifth and last question relates to a submission by the appellant that the Appeals Chamber should disregard Ambassador Scheffer's activities because he was merely prosecuting the foreign policy of his government and had no role to play in proceedings before the Tribunal. As has been noticed repeatedly, the Tribunal has no coercive machinery of its own. The Security Council sought to fill the gap by introducing a legal requirement for states to co-operate with the Tribunal. That obligation should not be construed so broadly as to constitute an unacceptable encroachment on the sovereignty of states; but it should certainly be interpreted in a manner which gives effect to the purposes of the Statute. I cannot think that anything in the purposes of the Statute prevents a state from using its good offices with another state to ensure that the needed cooperation of the latter with the Tribunal is forthcoming; on the contrary, those purposes would be consistent with that kind of *démarche*. Thus, accepting that Ambassador Scheffer was prosecuting the foreign policy of his

[61] See the statement in a previous case cited by Ritchie, J., in his leading opinion in *McMartin v. The Queen*, 1964 DLR LEXIS 1957, 46 DLR 2d 372. The statement related to "fresh evidence" but there is no reason why the principle involved cannot apply to new facts under the scheme of the Tribunal.

government, I cannot see that he was acting contrary to the principles of the Statute. Even if he was, I do not see that there was anything so inadmissibly incorrect in his activities as to outweigh the obvious relevance for this case of what he in fact did.

59. The statement of Judge Mballe of Cameroon is equally admissible as a new fact. It corroborates the substance of Ambassador Scheffer's statement in that it shows that, whatever was the reason, the delay was attributable to the decision-making process of the government of Cameroon; it was not the responsibility of the Tribunal or of any arm of the Tribunal.

(vi) The effect of the new facts

60. The appellant, along with others, was detained by Cameroon on an extradition request from Rwanda from 15 April 1996 to 21 February 1997. During that period of detention, he was also held by Cameroon at the request of the Prosecutor of the Tribunal for one month, from 17 April 1996 to 16 May 1996. In the words of the Appeals Chamber, on the latter day "the Prosecutor informed Cameroon that she only intended to pursue prosecutions against four of the detainees, *excluding* the Appellant".[62] Later, on "15 October 1996, responding to a letter from the Appellant complaining about his detention in Cameroon, the Prosecutor informed the Appellant that Cameroon was not holding him at her behest".[63] Today's judgment also shows that the appellant knew, at least by 3 May 1996, of the reasons for which he was held at the instance of the Prosecutor. These things being so, it appears to me that, from the point of view of proportionality, the Appeals Chamber focused on the subsequent period of detention at the request of the Tribunal, from 21 February 1997 to 19 November 1997, on which latter date the appellant was transferred from Cameroon to the Tribunal's detention unit in

---

[62] Decision of the Appeals Chamber, 3 November 1999, para. 5, original emphasis.
[63] Ibid., para. 7.

Arusha. How would the Appeals Chamber have viewed the appellant's detention during this period had it had the benefit of the new facts now available?

61. Regard being had to the jurisprudence, considered above, on the general judicial attitude to delay in the early phases of a criminal case, it is reasonable to hold that Rule 40*bis* contemplated a speedy transfer. If the transfer was effected speedily, no occasion would arise for considering whether the provision applied to extended detention in the place from which the transfer was to be made. In this case, the transfer was not effected speedily and the Appeals Chamber thought that the Tribunal (through the Prosecutor) was responsible for the delay, for which it accordingly looked for a remedy. In searching for this remedy, it is clear, from its decision read as a whole, that the central reason why it was moved to hold that the protection of that provision applied was because of its view that there was that responsibility. In this respect, I note that the appellant states that it "is the Prosecutor's failure to comply with the mandates of Rule 40 and Rule 40*bis* that compelled the Appeals Chamber to order the Appellant's release".[64] I consider that this implies that the appellant himself recognises that the real reason for the decision to release him was the finding by the Appeals Chamber that the Prosecutor (and, through her, the Tribunal) was responsible for the delay in Cameroon. It follows that if, as is shown by the statements of Ambassador Scheffer and Judge Mballe, the Tribunal was not responsible, the Appeals Chamber would not have had occasion to consider whether the provisions applied and whether the appellant should be released in accordance with Rule 40*bis*(H).

62. Thus, without disturbing the previous holding, made on the facts then known to the Appeals Chamber, that Rule 40*bis* was applicable to the Cameroon period (with which I do not agree), the conclusion is reached that, on the facts now known, the Appeals Chamber would not have held that the Rule applied to that period, with the

consequence that the Rule would not have been regarded as yielding the results which the Appeals Chamber thought it did.

63. Argument may be made on the basis of the previous holding (with which I disagreed) that Cameroon was the constructive agent of the Tribunal. On that basis, the contention could be raised that, even if the delay was caused by Cameroon and not by the Tribunal, the Tribunal was nonetheless responsible for the acts of Cameroon. However, assuming that there was constructive agency, such agency was for the limited purposes of custody pending speedy transfer. Cameroon could not be the Tribunal's constructive agent in respect of delay caused, as the new facts show, by Cameroon's acts over which the Tribunal had no control, which were not necessary for the purposes of the agency, and which in fact breached the purposes of the agency. Hence, even granted the argument of constructive agency, the new facts show that the Tribunal was not responsible for the delay as the Appeals Chamber thought it was on the basis of the facts earlier known to it.

64. There are other elements in the case, but that is the main one. Other new facts, mentioned in today's judgment, show that the violation of the appellant's rights in respect of delay between transfer and initial appearance was not as extensive as earlier thought; in any case, it did not involve the operation of a mandatory provision requiring release. The new facts also show that defence counsel acquiesced in the non-hearing of the habeas corpus motion on the ground that it had been overtaken by events. Moreover, as is also pointed out in the judgment, the matter has to be regulated by the approach taken by the Appeals Chamber in its decision of 3 November 1999. Paragraphs 106-109 of that decision made it clear that the conclusion reached was based not on a violation of any single right of the appellant but on an accumulation of violations of different rights. As

---

[64] Appellant's Response to Prosecutor's Motion for Review or Reconsideration, 17 February 2000, para.

has now been found, there are new facts which show that important rights which were thought to have been violated were not, and that accordingly there was not an accumulation of breaches. Consequently, the basis on which the Appeals Chamber ordered the appellant's release is displaced and the order for release vacated.

(vii) Conclusion

65. There are two closing reflections. One concerns the functions of the Prosecutor; the other concerns those of the Chambers.

66. As to her functions, the Prosecutor appeared to be of a mind that the independence of her office was invaded by a judicial decision that an indictment was dismissed and should not be brought back. She stated that she had "never seen" an instance of a prosecutor being prohibited by a court "from further prosecution ...".[65] In her submission, such a prohibition was at variance with her "completely independent" position and was "contrary to [her] duty as a prosecutor".[66] Different legal cultures are involved in the work of the Tribunal and it is right to try to understand those statements. It does appear to me, however, that the framework provided by the Statute of the Tribunal can be interpreted to accommodate the view of some legal systems that the independence of a prosecutor does not go so far as to preclude a court from determining that, in proper circumstances, an indicted person may be released and may not be prosecuted again for the same crime. The independence with which a function is to be exercised can be separated from the question whether the function is itself exercisable in a particular situation. A judicial determination as to whether the function may be exercised in a given situation is part of the relief that the court orders for a breach of the person's rights

36.
[65] Transcript, Appeals Chamber, 22 February 2000, p. 12.
[66] Ibid.

committed in the course of a previous exercise of those functions. This power of the courts has to be sparingly used; but it exists.

67. Also, the Prosecutor stated, in open court, that she had personally seen "5000 skulls" in Rwanda.[67] She said that the appellant was "responsible for the death of over ... 800,000 people in Rwanda, and the evidence is there. Irrefutable, incontrovertible, he is guilty. Give us the opportunity to bring him to justice."[68] Objecting on the basis of the presumption of innocence,[69] counsel for the appellant submitted that the Prosecutor had expressed herself in "a more aggressive manner than she should ..." and had "talked as if she was a depository of justice before" the Appeals Chamber.[70] I do not have the impression that the latter remark was entirely correct, but the differing postures did appear to throw up a question concerning the role of a prosecutor in an international criminal tribunal founded on the adversarial model. What is that role?

68. The Prosecutor of the ICTR is not required to be neutral in a case; she is a party. But she is not of course a partisan. This is why, for example, the Rules of the Tribunal require the Prosecutor to disclose to the defence all exculpatory material. The implications of that requirement suggest that, while a prosecution must be conducted vigorously, there is room for the injunction that prosecuting counsel "ought to bear themselves rather in the character of ministers of justice assisting in the administration of justice".[71] The prosecution takes the position that it would not prosecute without itself believing in guilt. The point of importance is that an assertion by the prosecution of its belief in guilt is not relevant to the proof. Judicial traditions vary and the Tribunal must seek to benefit from all of them. Taking due account of that circumstance, I nevertheless

---

[67] Ibid., p. 19.
[68] Ibid., p. 14.
[69] Ibid., p. 243.
[70] Ibid., pp. 138-139.

consider that the system of the Statute under which the Tribunal is functioning will support a distinction between an affirmation of guilt and an affirmation of preparedness to prove guilt. In this case, I would interpret what was said as intended to convey the latter meaning, but the strength with which the statements were made comes so close to the former that I consider it right to say that the framework of the Statute is sufficiently balanced and sufficiently stable not to be upset by the spirit of the injunction referred to concerning the role of a prosecutor. I believe that it is that spirit which underlies the remarks now made by the Appeals Chamber on the point.

69. As to the functions of the Chambers, whichever way it went, the decision in this case would call to mind that, on the second occasion on which *Pinochet's* case went to the British House of Lords, the presiding member of the Appellate Committee of the House noted that -

> [t]he hearing of this case ... produced an unprecedented degree of public interest not only in this country but worldwide. ... The conduct of Senator Pinochet and his regime have been highly contentious and emotive matters. ... This wide public interest was reflected in the very large number attending the hearings before the Appellate Committee including representatives of the world press. The Palace of Westminster was picketed throughout. The announcement of the final result gave rise to worldwide reactions.[72]

Naturally, however, (and as in this case), "the members of the Appellate Committee were in no doubt as to their function ...".[73]

70. Here too there has been interest worldwide, including a well-publicised suspension by Rwanda of cooperation between it and the Tribunal. On the one hand, the

---

[71] *R v Banks* [1916] 2 KB 621 at 623, per Avory J. In keeping with that view, it is indeed said that prosecuting counsel "should not regard himself as appearing for a party". See Code of Conduct of the Bar of England and Wales, para. 11(1).

[72] *R v Bow Street Metropolitan Stipendiary Magistrate and others, ex parte Pinochet Ugarte (No 2)*, [1999] 1 All ER 577, HL, at pp. 580-581, per Lord Browne-Wilkinson.

[73] Ibid.

appellant has asked the Appeals Chamber to "disregard ... the sharp political and media reaction to the decision, particularly emanating from the Government of Rwanda".[74] On the other hand, the Prosecutor has laid stress on the necessity for securing the cooperation of Rwanda, on the seriousness of the alleged crimes and on the interest of the international community in prosecuting them.

71. These positions have to be reconciled. How? This way: the sense of the international community has to be respectfully considered by an international court which does not dwell in the clouds; but that sense has to be collected in the whole. The interest of the international community in organising prosecutions is only half of its interest. The other half is this: such prosecutions are regarded by the international community as also designed to promote reconciliation and the restoration and maintenance of peace, but this is possible only if the proceedings are seen as transparently conforming to internationally recognised tenets of justice. The Tribunal is penal; it is not simply punitive.

72. It is believed that it was for this reason that the Security Council chose a judicial method in preference to other possible methods. The choice recalls the General Assembly's support for the 1985 Milan Resolution on Basic Principles on the Independence of the Judiciary, paragraph 2 of which reads: "The judiciary shall decide matters before them impartially, on the basis of facts and in accordance with the law, without any restrictions, improper influences, inducements, pressures, threats or interferences, direct or indirect, from any quarter or for any reason".[75] That text, to which counsel for the appellant appealed,[76] is a distant but clear echo of the claim that the law of Rome was "of a sort that cannot be bent by influence, or broken by power, or

---

[74] Defence Reply to the Prosecutor's Motion for Review or Reconsideration, 6 January 2000, para. 53.
[75] See General Assembly Resolution 40/32 of 29 November 1985, para. 1, General Assembly Resolution 40/146 of 13 December 1985, para. 2, and Seventh United Nations Congress on the Prevention of Crime and the Treatment of Offenders, Milan 26 August - 6 September 1985 (United Nations, New York, 1986), p. 60, para. 2.
[76] Transcript, Appeals Chamber, 22 February 2000, pp. 213-214.

spoilt by money". The timeless constancy of that ancient remark, cited for its substance rather than for its details, has in turn to be carried forward by a system of international humanitarian justice which was designed to function in the midst of powerful cross-currents of world opinion. Nor need this be as daunting a task as it sounds: it is easy enough if one holds on to the view that what the international community intended to institute was a system by which justice would be dispensed, not dispensed with.

73. But this view works both ways. In this case, there are new facts. These new facts both enable and require me to agree that justice itself has to regard the effect of the previous decision as now displaced; to adhere blindly to the earlier position in the light of what is now known would not be correct.

Done in both English and French, the English text being authoritative.

s/.

Mohamed Shahabuddeen

Dated this 31st day of March 2000
At The Hague
The Netherlands